# Berlitz®
# Greece

*Text by* John Chapple
*Edited by* Maria Lord
*Principal photographer:* Gregory Wrona
*Cover photograph by* Bill Bachman/Index/Powerstock
*Picture Editor:* Hilary Genin
*Managing Editor:* Tony Halliday

**Berlitz** POCKET GUIDE

# Greece

*First Edition 2003 (Reprinted 2004)*

**NO** part of this book may be reproduced, stored in a retrieval system or transmitted in any form or means electronic, mechanical, photocopying, recording or otherwise, without prior written permission from Berlitz Publishing. Brief text quotations with use of photographs are exempted for book review purposes only.

**PHOTOGRAPHY BY:**
Pete Bennett 20, 119, 120, 122, 123, 125, 133, 136, 141, 142; Andy Rouse/NHPA 76; Karen Van Dyke 23; Bill Wassman 21, 28, 30, 31, 32, 34, 37, 39, 41, 45, 46, 49, 50, 52; Phil Wood 10, 18, 71, 72, 75, 78, 82, 99, 100, 103, 104, 106; Gregory Wrona 1, 6, 8, 9, 12, 15, 17, 26, 38, 42, 44, 47, 48, 53, 56, 57, 58, 60, 61, 63, 65, 66, 67, 69, 74, 79, 81, 85, 86, 89, 90, 91, 93, 94, 96, 97, 107, 108, 110, 111, 112, 114/115, 117, 126, 128, 130, 135, 138, 145, 146

**CONTACTING THE EDITORS**
Every effort has been made to provide accurate information in this publication, but changes are inevitable. The publisher cannot be responsible for any resulting loss, inconvenience or injury. We would appreciate it if readers would call our attention to any errors or outdated information by contacting Berlitz Publishing, PO Box 7910, London SE1 1WE, England.
Fax: (44) 20 7403 0290;
e-mail: berlitz@apaguide.co.uk
www.berlitzpublishing.com

*All Rights Reserved*

© 2004 Apa Publications GmbH & Co.
Verlag KG, Singapore Branch, Singapore

*Printed in Singapore by Insight Print Services (Pte) Ltd, 38 Joo Koon Road, Singapore 628990.*
Tel: (65) 6865-1600. Fax: (65) 6861-6438

Berlitz Trademark Reg. U.S. Patent Office and other countries. Marca Registrada

➤
Crete (page 126), a world unto itself with breathtaking mountain scenery, beaches and a host of historical attractions

Corfu (page 97), a verdant island famous for its spring flowers and endless olive groves, distinctive for its Venetian heritage
▲

Santoríni (page 115), where 'sugar-cube' houses crown dramatic cliffs rising straight out of the Aegean ▼

# TOP TEN ATTRACTIONS

Metéora (page 58), where an astonishing ensemble of rock towers provide a holy retreat

◀ Métsovo (page 74), attractive mountain town and home to Greece's largest Vlach community

The Acropolis (page 28), a hub of classical Greek civilisation, including among its monuments the Parthenon, Propylaea and Erechtheion (pictured) ▶

Rhodes (page 122), largest of the Dodecanese Islands, stronghold of the medieval Knights of St John ▼

▶ Mystrás (page 89), a fascinating outpost of Byzantine culture

Delphi (page 59), important religious site of ancient Greece ▶

Mount Ólympos (page 85), Greece's highest mountain and ancient home to the gods ▶

# CONTENTS

*A ➤ in the text denotes a highly recommended sight*

## Fact Sheets

# GREECE AND THE GREEKS

For such a small country, Greece has played a large part in our collective history. The introduction of a form of democratic rule and the extraordinary intellectual and cultural achievements of the classical period (5th and 4th centuries BC) greatly influenced subsequent European history. Many physical remains of this period can be seen, largely in Athens but throughout the rest of the country as well. Remains from the later historical periods, Roman, Byzantine, Crusader and Ottoman rule also can be seen, layer upon historical layer, in this wonderfully complex land.

## Modernity and Tradition

Most visitors, with classical Greece in mind, are surprised by contemporary Greece. It is a thriving modern country with a diverse and growing economy. The repressive 1967–74 dictatorship of the Colonels *(see page 23)* is long gone. The EU has provided much of the money being spent on the country's infrastructure, which is evident primarily in the road system. More importantly, EU membership has brought a sense of security the modern country has never had concerning her borders, primarily with Turkey. Greece's long and tumultuous relations with Turkey have been good in recent years, but there have been difficulties, and it is comforting to know that Greece's borders now are the borders of the EU.

For all their EU membership, the Greeks are eastern Mediterranean through and through. This can be startling to visitors who think Europe is homogenised or first think of Greece in terms of its classical past. We are not taught about the highly individual nature of modern Greeks. While enjoying

**Aegean blue and white at the harbour of Sitía**

**The interior of Greece is largely mountainous**

their often kind and warm hospitality, visitors to Greece today can examine the early history of settled Europeans, often in beautiful locations; consider the complications of Greece's medieval and modern history; enjoy some lovely wildlife habitats; or opt for the pleasures of sea, sand and mountains.

For most visitors, Athens is the first destination, a large urban sprawl containing close to 3 million people in the city's greater urban area, some 27 percent of the country's 10.9 million population. Athens has wonderful archaeological sites and Byzantine churches, fascinating museums, and a thriving cultural life most easily available to non-Greek speaking visitors through many art galleries and musical performances. It also has some fine restaurants, including a myriad of *tavérnes* well worth visiting for their informal atmosphere and good Greek food.

Several ancient sites are outside Athens but within Attica. The most famous are the Temple of Poseidon at Sounion dramatically perched on a cliff at the southernmost end of Attica and, northeast of Athens, Marathon, where the ancient city-state of Athens defeated the Persian Empire in 490BC. These, and other small gems such as Brauron, Amphiareion and Rhamnous are within comfortable reach by car.

## The Islands

For all the pleasures and history of Athens and Attica, the country's real beauty is outside the major cities. The different groups of islands are an obvious draw, starting with the four main Argo-Saronic Islands almost within commuting distance from Piraeus. Ídhra and Spétses are the two best known, Spétses more wooded and Ídhra with its beautiful little port, both major players in the early 19th century Greek struggle for independence. Now they are havens for Athenians wanting comfortable summer homes easily accessible from Athens. It takes only half an hour on a hydrofoil to reach the closest, Égina, so some people do, in fact, commute from the island to work in Piraeus or Athens every day.

The Cycladic Islands, the large circular island group in the central Aegean, have received much attention because of their white, almost cubistic architecture, often limited vegetation, and crystalline sea. This apparent reduction to basic elements, best known on Mýkonos, is dramatic and appealing, but there is considerable variation in the Cyclades. Náxos, for example, is mountainous inland, very green, and its farms are productive. Kéa, just under 1½hrs by ferry

**Café culture in Thessaloníki**

from Lávrion, the Attica port near Sounion, has both green valleys and bare shores and its one village is a collection of white houses set high on the mountain.

Three of the Dodecanese Islands have calm volcanic activity (Kós, Nísyros, Santoríni), but all retain varying degrees of influence from Crusader and Ottoman and Italian rule. The Sporades Islands, further north, are wonderful mixtures of green vegetation and fine beaches. The Ionian Islands, heavily influenced by some 300 years of Italian rule, are the greenest of all, for rain clouds generally enter Greece from the northwest and release much of their water when they arrive. All the islands, are unique unto themselves, as are the Greeks, and those living on these islands have strong local traditions and the tenacious belief that their particular island is the best place on earth.

**A Byzantine mosaic from Néa Moní, Híos**

## Environment

The country's 131,949 sq km (50,950 sq miles) are astonishingly diverse, with beaches, forests, and much else environmentally. There are more species of wildflowers in Greece than any other country in Western Europe. In spring some fields are blanketed with colour, including wild orchids, and in the autumn you will see bunches of cyclamen along with wild crocuses, to name only a very few. The country is also a haven for many species of birds, some of them on the international list of endangered species. The Préspes Lakes, Lake Kastoriá, the Évros Delta and Lake Kerkíni, all in northern Greece, are just the best-known of the country's ten Ramsar wetlands, providing safe habitats for rare waterfowl such as the Dalmatian Pelican. The Dhadiá Forest, also in northern Greece, is an impressive refuge for raptors, including several rare species and the huge Black Vulture, with a 3-m (10-ft) wingspan.

## The Greek Orthodox Church

The Church in Greece occupies a special place in the conciousness of the nation. One of the few established Churches in Europe, until recently membership of the Orthodox Church was considered the essential mark of 'Greekness' and of belonging to the nation. The Church's roots lie in the Byzantine Empire and the Church of Constantine established in Constantinople (present-day Istanbul). The city remained the seat of power until it fell to the Ottomans in 1453.

Even if it were no longer part of a theocratic government, Orthodoxy was tolerated by the Muslim Ottomans and for the next 400 years the Church became the preserver of the Greek identity and language. Village-based Greek society looked to it for education and, from the 18th century onwards, as a rallying point for a growing national conciousness. The church played a considerable part in the War of Independence and was rewarded by taking a central role in the development of the new state.

While the Church has traditionally been a focus for Greek life, its influence is on the wane. It has become increasingly concerned with topics of little importance to the majority of Greeks; the most it has been able to rouse itself recently has been over the issue of identity cards, and whether they should state the carrier's religion.

## A BRIEF HISTORY

The earliest settled communities in Greece date to about 6000BC, the beginning of the neolithic era, when the domestication of animals and the cultivation of grain arrived from the east. Soon after 3000BC societies able to produce bronze weapons and tools arose in the Cyclades Islands and Crete. During this early Bronze Age olives and grapes began to be cultivated, and remain staples of Greek agriculture. In around 2000BC another group of people brought the horse, the potter's wheel, and the Greek language. These Late Bronze Age or Mycenaean societies are familiar to us from Greek myths and legends.

Theories involving invasions, earthquakes, drought or revolution have been put forward, but it is not known why

**Grave circle A at Mycenae**

the palaces and social systems of Bronze-Age life in Greece were destroyed in approximately 1100BC. The following 300 years are the so-called 'Dark Ages'. Iron, much stronger than bronze for tools and weapons, was introduced, but society seems to have been fragmented, with few signs of material wealth and only very simple housing.

## City-States

In the 8th century BC the country began to reorganise, and trade developed with other parts of the eastern Mediterranean. Writing, which had been lost, was reintroduced, probably from Phoenicia. The emerging political organisation became based not on palaces but on city-states; these included Athens, which came to occupy the peninsula of Attica, a total of 3,885 sq km (1,500 sq miles).

Agamemnon, King of Mycenae, is known to us through Homer's *Iliad* and the *Oresteia* of Aeschylus. He waged war on Troy, and on his return was murdered by his wife, Clytemnestra.

The model of localised political development owes much to Greece's geography: the country's mountainous terrain, isolated valleys and numerous islands encouraged the formation of local centres of power. Many city-states sent out waves of colonisation that spread Greek culture throughout the Mediterranean and up into the Black Sea. Politically, most city-states passed through periods of rule by monarchy, aristocracy, tyranny and democracy. In Athens the move towards democracy began late in the 6th century BC.

## Persian Wars

When the Greek city-states in Ionia revolted against Persian rule in 499BC, Athens sent a fleet to help, and in the following year the insurgents sacked the Persian city of Sardis. The Persians eventually quelled the revolt and then moved against

Greece. After taking over northern Greece, they moved down to attack Athens in 490BC, landing at Marathon. The Spartans had refused a request for help, so the Athenians, with only a small contingent of Plataeans as allies, fought and routed the far more numerous Persian army.

Ten years later the Persians, under Xerxes, invaded Greece again. They gained control of the north and central areas and, after overcoming the heroic defence of the pass at Thermopylae by the Spartans, occupied an abandoned Athens, where they destroyed the temples on the Acropolis. The Greek fleet had withdrawn to Salamis, where they tricked the Persians into a battle when the Persians were exhausted and the Greeks rested. This victory left the Greeks in command of the seas. In 479BC, the Persian army was defeated by Sparta at Plataea.

## The Laws of Solon

Solon was appointed leader of Athens in 594BC to mediate and draw up new laws in the face of economic distress and political unrest that had not been quelled by the Draconian laws (circa 624BC). These had established a degree of legal security, but had not recognised the role played by the fluctuation of social and economic status in the politics and rule of the city. Solon's achievement was to acknowledge this movement in the social and economic order, and he attempted to impose order with a move towards a form of representative democracy. He cancelled all debts for which land or liberty could be forfeited, established a new court of law to which all citizens could appeal, divided the population into four classes according to income, and ruled that people holding government office were to come from the wealthier classes. A new council (boule) was established of 400 members to formulate proposals discussed in the full assembly of adult male citizens. However, it was not until Cleisthenes received enough popular support to make further reforms in 508BC, that political unrest was finally quashed.

# The Classical Period

Following the defeat of the Persians, Greek power was divided between Athens and Sparta. Many small city states in Asia Minor still felt threatened by the Persians and turned to Athens, as the dominant naval power, for protection. In 478BC the states formed the Delian League (after the island of Delos where the meeting took place). City-states in the south of Greece allied themselves with Sparta, which was becoming wary of the Athenian build-up of power and influence.

Athens levied taxes on the league for its navy, and money poured into the city. With the rule of Pericles (461BC onwards), this was invested in building (notably on the Acropolis) and the arts. This was the beginning of the great flowering of Athenian culture that saw the writings of Sophocles, Aeschylus and Euripides, the ideas of philosophers Plato and Socrates and the works of sculptors Pheidias and Praxiteles.

**The classical theatre at Epídavros**

In the sphere of politics, Pericles turned his attention towards Sparta, and formed an alliance with Argos. Sparta, suspicious of this joining of rival powers, started the First Peloponnesian War against Athens, which it believed it would quickly win. Sparta was mistaken, and Athens dominated during the early years of the war. However, after a disastrous campaign in Egypt, Pericles negotiated a 30-year peace with Sparta in 445BC.

As part of the peace, Athens had given up power over states on the mainland, while Sparta recognised the Athenian

Empire. However, Athens continued to build up its power, especially after transferring the treasury from Delos to Athens, and in 431BC the Second Peloponnesian War broke out. In 404BC the Spartans, with help from the Persians, finally defeated Athens, bringing an end to the Athenian 'golden age'.

## Hellenistic and Roman Rule

Spartan hegemony lasted until 371BC, when it was supplanted by the Thebans, before Athens regained the upper hand in 355BC. In 338BC the rising power of the Macedonian kingdom under Philip II turned its attention towards the south. Athens and Thebes, now allied against the common threat, were defeated at Chaironeia in Boeotia north of Attica and Philip became the ruler of mainland Greece. Philip's rule of Athens was benign, as was that of his son Alexander the Great, and the city flourished despite strong local resentment against Macedonian rule. After the death of Alexander in 323BC, Athens became largely a pawn in the political conflicts of others, but the city was respected for its illustrious past and continuing role as a university centre to the ancient world.

> Alexander the Great is a controversial figure. Some see him as the greatest general in history, others as a bloodthirsty tyrant. Whatever the truth of these competing claims (and they are not mutually exclusive) he did rule over the largest empire of the ancient world, stretching from Greece to India.

The Romans continued supporting the city after taking control of Greece in 146BC. In 86BC the Athenians supported the revolt by Mithridates against Rome, causing the Romans to attack and capture the city. Athens misjudged again and supported Antony against Octavian (later Augustus) before the great naval battle of Actium in 31BC.

Nonetheless, prominent Romans came to Athens to study and Roman rulers, from Julius Caesar on, paid for new buildings. To take only two examples, Julius Caesar began the construction of the Roman Agora just east of the Athenian Agora, and Hadrian (AD117–138) built the Library of Hadrian and the Pantheon.

During the 3rd century disaster struck in the form of an attack by the Herulians, a Germanic tribe who came south from the Black Sea to wreak havoc in Greece. They sacked and burned Athens in AD267 and then moved on to sack Corinth, Sparta and Argos before they were annihilated by the Byzantine imperial army in AD269.

## Byzantine Period

With the establishment of the city of Constantinople in AD330 the Roman Empire became divided into eastern and

**A frieze from the Roman Arch of Galerius, Thessaloníki**

**A Byzantine ceiling at Mystrás**

western sectors. Rome was to fall to successive waves of barbarian invaders, but Constantinople grew to thrive as the capital of the Byzantine Empire (395–1453). Athens continued to serve as the great educational and cultural centre until AD529, when the conservative religious Christian emperor Justinian ordered that the pagan philosophical schools in Athens be closed, ending a tradition of 1,000 years and consigning Athens to obscurity.

Christianity played a pivotal role in the establishment of Constantinople and continued to do so in the daily lives of all Greeks in the Byzantine Empire. The major buildings erected in Athens and Thessaloníki during the Byzantine period were churches, many of which are still standing in their Pláka and Kástra districts. In 1204 the Fourth Crusade decided against attacking Muslims in the Holy Land and attacked the Christian Byzantine Empire instead. Athens fell to Othon de la Roche, whose son Guy was given the title of

Duke of Athens in 1225. Athens did not prosper during this period of rule by French crusaders, which ended in 1311 when the Catalan Company took over the city. The Catalans, in turn, were defeated in 1387 when Nerio Acciajuoli, the Florentine lord of Corinth, captured Athens.

Byzantium's decline had one brief final flowering in the mid-13th century when the centre of power moved to Mystrás in the southern Peloponnese. After the fall of Constantinople to the Ottomans in 1453, Mystrás became the last outpost of the empire, holding out until 1460.

## Ottoman Rule – Venetian Occupation

The Ottoman army continued to move west after 1453, and arrived in Athens in 1456, although the last Acciajuoli duke of Athens did not surrender the Acropolis until 1458. The Turks made the Acropolis a Turkish town, forbidding entry to Christians. Many Albanians, who had served as mercenary troops for both the Byzantines and the Ottomans, moved to Athens and settled in Pláka.

Under Ottoman rule, which quickly spread across much of Greece, many places acquired mosques; those still standing include the Fethiye mosque in Athens and the large mosques in Ioánnina and on Kós. The Ottomans also transformed a number of churches into mosques, including the Parthenon on the Acropolis. Everyday life for the majority of Greeks under Ottoman rule changed little. There was a high degree of religious tolerance, and the Orthodox Church became the effective religious and civil ruler of the Christian Greek populations of the empire.

Ottoman rule did not extend over the entirety of Greece and a few areas, in particular the Ionian and Cycladic islands, were held by the Venetians. Skirmishes abounded between the Venetians and the Ottomans (the Venetians took over Athens between 1687–8), and later, briefly, the revolutionary French.

By the 18th century opposition to Ottoman rule was building. As well as challenges from local rulers such as Ali Pasha *(see page 68)*, secret societies, notably the Filikí Etería based outside of Greece, supported bands of freedom fighters.

## War of Independence – Independent Greece

The Greek War of Independence began in the Peloponnese in 1821, and in 1822 the Athenians expelled the Turks from Athens. Ottoman forces returned, however, in 1826 to besiege the city, and in June of 1827 they captured the Acropolis. The Greeks were obliged to sign a treaty turning Athens over to the Turks, after which the Greeks retired to the island of Salamína. The real issue was decided, however, a few months later when, on 20 October 1827 a combined British, French and Russian fleet defeated the Turko-Egyptian fleet at Navarino on the west coast of the Peloponnese. In 1830 the London Protocol was signed by the 'Great Powers' of Britain, France, Russia and the Ottoman Empire, recognising Greece as an independent kingdom.

**The mosque on Kós**

The transition to independent government was not smooth. The first president of Greece, Ioannis Kapodistrias, was killed in Náfplio in 1831. Otto of Bavaria was made King of Greece in

1832, and the last Turkish troops on the Acropolis surrendered in February 1833. In September 1834 Athens was officially declared the capital of Greece. At the time, the city was little more than a village, with a population of 4,000. During the classical period the population had been 36,000.

**The Greek flag on the Acropolis**

## Balkan Wars – New Lands

The Balkan Wars (1912–13) drastically reduced the amount of territory the fading Ottoman Empire controlled in the Balkans. In terms of how these wars affected Greece, the basic events were that Greece, Serbia, Romania and Bulgaria allied against Turkey. The Greeks drove the Turks from what is now northern Greece and Epirus in the first Balkan War and then, in the second Balkan War, drove the Bulgarians out of Thrace and Macedonia. Greece gained Epirus, Macedonia, and Thrace, including the cities of Ioánnina, Kavála, and Thessaloníki, and the islands of Sámos and Crete. These territorial gains almost doubled the size of the country.

## World War I – the Catastrophe

After a long political struggle between King Constantine, who wanted Greece to remain neutral during World War I, and Prime Minister Venizelos, who wanted Greece to join the Allies, Greece formally joined the Allies in 1917.

The Allies, notably the British under Prime Minister Lloyd George, had promised Greece the city of Smyrna (modern Izmir) and its hinterland as an enticement to join the war effort against Germany and Austria (with whom the Turks were allied). Many Greeks were living in this area, descendants of ancient Greek colonists who had settled on the coast of Asia Minor in the 7th century BC, but they were not a majority. Greek troops, acting on Venizelos's orders, invaded Turkey in 1919.

The Greek invasion ignited Turkish nationalism, led by Mustafa Kemal, who fought the Greek army to a year-long standstill and then turned the tide. After defeating the Greek forces the Turks then expelled the Greek populations living throughout Turkey (except Istanbul), killing large numbers of Greeks in the process. In the ensuing exchange of populations, approximately 380,000 Muslims moved from Greece to Turkey and over a million Greeks moved from western Turkey and eastern Thrace to Greece. The disaster was so overwhelming for the Greeks that they still refer to it as the Catastrophe, and it turned their collective attention firmly to the West.

> A catastrophic and powerful current running through Greek politics in the 19th and early-20th century was the Megáli Idhéa ('Great Idea'), to restore the boundaries of the old Byzantine Empire.

## World War II

Social inequalities expressed in labour unrest gave General Metaxas an excuse to impose a dictatorship in 1936. His Fascist sympathies are reviled, but nonetheless Metaxas is best remembered for standing up to Fascist Italy. On 28 October 1940, Mussolini sent a humiliating ultimatum, which Metaxas rejected out of hand. The bluntness of his rejection has been popularised as 'Óhi' (No), and October 28 is celebrated each year as Óhi Day. The Greek army, enthusiastically supported throughout the country, stopped the invading Italian forces north of Ioánnina and drove them back into Albania. It was a David and Goliath victory, but was nullified by the German invasion in April of 1941. Greek, and British and Australian, forces defending the country were driven south to Crete, where they were defeated in a fiercely fought battle in late May. The German occupation of Greece was heavy handed, with severe reprisals carried out in response to acts of Greek resistance, and the Germans systematically looted the country of whatever they could find of value. Particularly during the winter of 1941–2 in Athens, many Greeks died of starvation.

## Civil War

When the war ended in the autumn of 1944, German troops withdrew, most of them to be captured or killed as they retreated through Yugoslavia, but civil war erupted in December of 1944. The contesting sides were the Communists, who had controlled much of the territory not under direct German control during the war, and the royalist Greek government. The US provided military and financial support to the Greek government, which finally defeated the communist forces in 1949.

**An anti-Colonels poster**

## The Junta

In the spring of 1967 an army colonel named George Papadopoulos led a *coup d'etat* and took over the country. The young King Constantine first welcomed the junta and then botched a counter-coup against them, succeeding only in being forced into exile. The junta used arrest and torture to control dissent, making the Greeks increasingly unhappy with the junta's ridiculous claims to be healing a sick society. In 1973, when students occupied university buildings in Athens, Pátra, and Thessaloníki in demonstration against the junta, public support was strong. The junta answered with troops, arrested 1,000 people, and, in the process, killed at least 34 students.

People throughout the country were horrified by the slaughter, but the junta responded only with an internal coup, replacing Colonel Papadopoulos with the even more hard-line Brigadier Ioannidis. Ioannidis decided to settle a long-simmering feud with Bishop Makarios, the president of Cyprus, by organising a coup against him in the summer of 1974. The Turks responded to Greek military activity in Cyprus by occupying approximately one third of the island. This humiliation was too much for the Greek army, which deposed the junta in July of 1974 and turned the country back over to civilian rule.

## Contemporary Greece

Life in Greece has been improving steadily ever since. The monarchy was ended by referendum in 1976. In 1981 Greece became the 10th member of the EU, becoming fully integrated at the end of 1993 and joining the single European currency in 2002. All elections held since 1974 have been, fundamentally, a contest between the centre right party, Néa Dhimokratía, founded by Konstantinos Karamanlis, and the centre left party, PASOK, founded by the politically formidable Andreas Papandreou. Although the balance of power is finely divided between the two, whichever party is in power, Greece is now politically stable with a sizable economy.

# Historical Landmarks

*circa* **6000**BC Domestication of animals, grain cultivation.

**3000**BC Early Bronze Age on Cyclades and Crete.

**2000**BC Mycenaean civilization.

*circa* **1100**BC Fall of Mycenaean civilization.

**1100–800**BC 'Dark Ages', arrival of iron tools.

**8th century** BC Development of city-states.

**490–479**BC The Persian Wars

**479–323**BC Classical Period.

**432–404**BC The Peloponnesian Wars.

**338**BC Athens defeated by Philip of Macedonia.

**323**BC**–146**BC Hellenistic Period.

**146**BC Romans occupy Greece.

**1225–1456** Crusader dynasties rule Athens.

**1453** Ottoman Turks capture Constantinople.

**1456** Ottoman Turks occupy most of Greece.

**1687** Turko-Venetian War.

**1821** Start of Greek War of Independence.

**1827** Turko-Egyptian fleet defeated by the 'Great Powers'.

**1834** Athens made capital of independent Greece.

**1912–13** Balkan Wars.

**1919** Greek troops enter Smyrna.

**1921** Greek advance towards Ankara stopped by Turkish army.

**1922** The Catastrophe. Over one million Greeks expelled from Turkey.

**1936** General Ioannis Metaxas imposes dictatorship upon Greece.

**1940** Italian invasion stopped by Greek army.

**1941–44** German military occupation of Greece.

**1944–49** Greek Civil War.

**1967–74** Military junta rules Greece.

**1976** Referendum ends Greek monarchy.

**1981** Greece joins EU.

**2002** Greece adopts the euro as its currency.

**2004** The Olympic Games are held in Athens.

# WHERE TO GO

## GETTING AROUND

W here to go depends upon personal preference, for the choices are myriad. The mainland and the Peloponnese have sites from all periods of Greece's history as well as some extraordinarily beautiful locations. Public transport is comprehensive and a convenient way to travel. If beaches are your thing, head for the islands.

The country's three basic divisions are the mainland, the Peloponnese, and the islands. The mainland consists of several distinct areas, including Athens and Attica in the southeast; Central Greece, including Thessaly; Epirus in the northwest; and, in northern Greece, Macedonia and Thrace. The huge almost-island of the Peloponnese is south. The Aegean Islands consist of six island groups, starting with the Argo-Saronic Gulf Islands near Athens, the Cyclades, the Sporades, the Dodecanese, and the Northern and Eastern Aegean Islands. Crete is south of the Cyclades and the Ionian Islands are along the country's western coast, ending with Kýthira and Andikýthira north of Crete.

## ATHENS

The country's capital is a fascinating mix of ancient and modern, classical and Byzantine, the run-down and the chic. Many visitors pass through quickly, catching the Acropolis and a couple of museums en-route, before heading off to the islands or other sights on the mainland. However, Athens more than repays a longer stay. Quite apart from the ancient sites and museums, it gives a picture of modern Greece all too often ignored in favour of a picture-postcard view of the country.

**The spectacular monasteries of Metéora**

## The Acropolis

Athens lies between two lines of mountains, Hymettos (Ymettó) to the east and Párnitha to the west on a largely gentle plain sloping down to the sea. The plain is dramatically interrupted by three decreasing hills, of which the smallest and best known is the **Acropolis** (open daily 8am–7pm, admission fee).

At the top of the steeply inclined entrance is the **Propylaia**, the commanding gateway to the Acropolis, built immediately after the Parthenon, in 437–432BC. To the right was the small **Temple of Athena Niké**, completed in around 424BC. One of the two versions of the Aegeus myth culminates here. Theseus had promised his father, Aegeus, that he would return with white sails on his ships if he overcame the Minotaur on Crete, a promise he forgot. His father, seeing the black sails from the Acropolis, believed his son to be dead and threw himself into the sea – called Aegean after him – and died.

The view of the sanctuary from the Propylaia is still impressive. In front was the **statue of Athena Promachos** made by Pheidias in approximately 460BC. This bronze statue was so tall that the reflection of the helmet and spear could be seen by ships at sea. The route from here to the

**The Propylaia from below**

Parthenon's entrance at the far eastern end of the temple, over what today is barren rock, was lined with innumerable shrines, most of them sculptures, to gods and heroes.

The **Parthenon** dominates the Acropolis (see box opposite). The pedimental sculptures left after the disastrous explosion caused by Venetian shelling in 1687 were carted off to London by Lord Elgin in the first decade of the 19th century. Those that survived the process of being taken down, and the journey, are on display in the British Museum, much to the chagrin of the Greeks.

The **Erechtheion** was built in the years 421–406BC on the site Athenians associate with the contest between Poseidon and Athena for the city. The ancient builders left a hole in the

---

## The Parthenon

The name Parthenon comes from the huge statue by Pheidias of Athena Parthenos, inside the temple. Nothing of this huge gold and ivory statue remains, but a small Roman copy is in the National Archaeological Museum. The building was erected between 447 and 438BC, although the sculptural decorations were not completed until 432BC. There may have been an archaic temple on the site that was pulled down to make room for what is referred to as the Older Parthenon, on which work began a few years after the Athenians defeated the Persians at Marathon in 490BC. When the Persians occupied and burned Athens in 480BC they destroyed everything on the Acropolis. The Athenians vowed not to rebuild the desecrated shrines and temples, but after 33 years they adopted the plan proposed by Pericles for major temple construction.

Only marble from Mt Pentéli was used for building and all available space was filled with sculptural decoration. There were 17 Doric columns along each side and eight instead of the usual six at each end. The columns are narrower and set more closely together than usual, giving an impression of solidity in contrast to the large central room, or *cella*. The *cella* was large enough to accommodate the 11-m (36-ft) high statue of Athena. The architecture is extraordinarily subtle. The stepped platform on which the Parthenon rests is slightly curved to offset any visual distortion, seen easily by standing outside the northeastern corner and looking along its northern line.

ceiling of the northern porch to show where Poseidon's trident came to make the salt spring gush forth. They also left a hole in the floor so visitors could look down and see the marks the trident made in the rock. Today the site is roped off, but the holes in the roof and the floor can easily be seen.

The southern porch – the **Caryatid Porch** – is named after the six draped maidens, one and a half times life size, supporting the porch roof (all the ones we see today are modern copies). One Caryatid was removed during the Ottoman occupation and has since disappeared and another, now in the British Museum, was taken by Lord Elgin. The four remaining originals are in the Acropolis Museum.

The area west of the Erechtheion was also sacred ground. An altar to Zeus was said to have been beneath the olive tree by which Athena won the contest for the city. According to Herodotus, Athena's olive tree was burned down during the

**Pheidias' masterpiece, the Parthenon**

Persian sack of the Acropolis
but fresh shoots grew from
the old trunk. The tree was
still standing in the 1st century AD. An olive tree, albeit a
modern one, grows on the
same spot today.

In the southeastern corner
of the Acropolis, the **Acropolis Museum** (open Tues–Sun
8am–7pm, Mon 11am–7pm)
contains impressive archaic
and classical remains,

**The Erechtheion Caryatids**

including the Caryatids and an archaic statue of a young
man, *kouros*, carrying a calf across his shoulders (570BC).

## The Areopagos

The rocky hill below the Acropolis to the northwest, to the
right and down the slope as you leave the Acropolis
entrance, is the **Areopagos**, the Hill of Ares, on which was
held a court of justice, the Council of the Areopagos, set up
to deliberate on major crimes. The name comes from the
mythical Ares, the god of war, who was tried here – and
acquitted – after having killed Halirrhotios, a son of the sea
god Poseidon, after he had become involved with Ares' own
daughter, Alkippe.

The Council of the Areopagos also had jurisdiction over
constitutional and religious matters, so when St Paul visited
Athens in AD49 with 'new teaching' he was summoned to
appear before it. The Greek text of his speech (Acts
17:22–31) is inscribed on a large plaque on the east side of
the extremely slippery steps climbing the Areopagos. Dionysios the Areopagite became St Paul's first Athenian convert,
and St Dionysios is the patron saint of Athens.

**The Stoa of Attalos**

## The Agora

The Acropolis was fundamentally for religious activities, but the **Ancient Greek Agora** (open daily 8am–7pm; admission fee) was for virtually all public purposes. In ancient Greek the word *agora* meant gathering place and this was the centre of Athenian life.

What you see here today are the remains of many different periods of life in the Agora. The buildings of the archaic Agora were in the west below the hill of Kolonos Agoraios (Market Hill), graced since the middle of the 5th century BC by the **Hephaisteion**. This Doric temple was dedicated to Hephaistos and Athena and is the best-preserved ancient Greek temple in the world. When leaving the Hephaisteion, walk to your right, south, along the paved path until you come to an open area with a large reconstructed site plan displayed in a case. This gives a clear view of the Agora, together with an impression of what it looked like in AD150.

Political reforms establishing democracy were instituted in 507–8BC. These reforms gave birth to the senate, which consisted of 500 Athenians who served for one year and met daily except during festivals in the **Old Bouleuterion**, just below the southeastern corner of the Hephaisteion. (The assembly of all citizens met about every 10 days on the Pnyx.)

When the Persians occupied Athens in 480BC they destroyed all they could in the Agora as well as on the Acropolis. After the Persian defeat in 479BC the Athenians built the

**Painted** or **Poikile Stoa** and the **Tholos**, along with other projects, and rebuilt the **Royal Stoa** and the Old Bouleuterion, all on the west side of the Agora.

The **Panathenaic Way** is now visible as the wide diagonal path running through the Agora from below the lower entrance just across the tram line up past the southwestern corner of the Stoa of Attalos towards the Acropolis. It was used for theatrical presentations and various athletic events that were viewed by spectators from temporary wooden stands.

The **Stoa of Attalos** was built in the 2nd century BC by King Attalos II of Pergamum (159–138BC) in Asia Minor. Apparently, he had so enjoyed his time studying in Athens during his youth that he built the huge shopping arcade on the east side of the Agora as a gift to the city. Reconstructed in

---

## Panathenaic Festival

The Panathenaic Festival seems to have been held since Mycenaean times. In 566BC it was reorganised to include the Greater Panathenaic Festival, perhaps the most important of the city's religious festivals. The festival's central act was bringing a newly woven cloth to dress the statue of Athena Polias, the protector of the city. Until the Persians destroyed the temple in 480BC the statue was an ancient wooden sculpture housed in the Old Temple of Athena. When the Parthenon was built the replacement was made of gold and ivory. Every four years the new dress was placed on the mast of a wooden ship on wheels that was then pulled from the Dipylon Gate (in what is now the Kerameikos archaeological site, about 500m/550yds west on Ermou Street) along the Panathenaic Way through the ancient Greek Agora until the ascent became too steep. The dress was then carried on foot up to the Acropolis and placed on the statue. Many other activities, such as plays and athletic contests, were associated with the festival.

**One of the Odeion's Tritons**

the 1950s, it now contains the fascinating Agora Museum *(see below)*.

The Romans filled the large open central space with the **Temple of Ares** and the much larger **Odeion (concert hall) of Agrippa**. The Temple of Ares was, in fact, a 5th-century BC temple dismantled and moved from its original, unknown, site and re-erected here in the Agora during the reign of Augustus.

The enormous Odeion of Agrippa, probably completed by 12BC, was at least three storeys high and could seat 1,000 people. After 150 years the 25-m (82-ft) unsupported span of the Odeion roof collapsed. It was reconstructed with an interior wall supporting the roof, cutting by half the seating capacity of the auditorium. The remodelling included the huge **Giants** (half man, half snake) and **Tritons** (half man, half fish), which so command attention when you enter the Agora from Adrianou Street.

## The Agora Museum

The museum (open Tues–Sun 8am–7pm, Mon 11am–7pm), on the ground floor of the Stoa of Attalos, is one long room taking up what would have been space for 10 ancient shops. It displays representative finds from 5,000 years of Athenian history, some of the most interesting being the bronze ballots, the allotment machine and *ostraka* (inscribed potsherds).

The bronze ballots are small wheels with axles produced by the city for determining votes by juries. If the axles were solid the vote was for acquittal, if hollow the vote was for conviction. Each juror was given a ballot with a hollow and a solid axle, which he held between thumb and forefinger so his vote would be secret.

The marble allotment machine determined the composition of juries. Each juror was issued a bronze ticket that was put into a slot in the machine. A hollow tube contained a random mixture of black and white balls, and a crank at the bottom of the machine released a single ball. If the first ball were white, then all the jurors from the first row were selected, if the second ball were black then the jurors on the second row were free, and so on.

*Ostraka*, the origin of our word ostracism, are potsherds. Every year the Athenians voted by scratching on *ostraka* the name of any individual they thought was becoming too powerful and might become a tyrant. If a majority of the required 6,000 votes cast had one name, the individual named would be exiled from Athens for 10 years.

> The Hephaisteion is also known as the Thiseon (as is the nearby metro station) because the temple's frieze and metopes depicted the exploits of the Athenian hero, Theseus.

## The Pnyx

The law courts and the representative assembly met in the Agora, but the full assembly of all citizens met every 10 days on the **Pnyx**, the central of three heights west of the Acropolis and Agora, to vote on laws proposed by the senate. For votes to be valid, a minimum of 6,000 citizens (men only; women, children and slaves did not vote) met in the curved slope of the hill overlooking the Agora and the Acropolis. Today the Pnyx is fenced off.

## The Kerameikos Cemetery

The main cemetery of ancient Athens is in the area known as the **Kerameikos** (open daily 8am–7pm; admission fee) about 400m (¼ mile) from the ancient Greek Agora.

In the archaeological site today we can see substantial remains of the city walls and two gates, the Sacred Gate and the Dipylon Gate. The **Sacred Gate** led on to the **Sacred Way**, named because the annual procession from Eleusis, celebrating Demeter's descent into the Underworld in search of her daughter Persephone, came along this road and through this gate. About 55m (50 yds) further on are the remains of the **Dipylon Gate**, which was built in 479BC, and rebuilt at the end of the 4th century. This was the main gate into the city for those travelling on a route that was known as Dromos ('road') outside the walls, and the Panathenaic Way inside. A modern cement path runs between the remains of the two massive square outer towers of the gate. It was the largest gate in ancient Greece – 20m (22yds) across and 37m (41 yds) deep, creating a large courtyard in which attackers were subjected to fire from high walls on three sides. Close by is the **Pompeion**, a building where the sacred items for the Panathenaic procession were stored.

> Few places in Athens can be called a habitat for anything other than humans. However, inside the entrance to the archaeological site a sign in Greek states that the Kerameikos is both a habitat and an archaeological site and asks visitors not to bother the turtles or frogs there.

The city's honoured dead were buried at public expense along the Dromos, the road which led to the Academy from the Dipylon Gate, but there is little to be seen of these graves today. More graves, many of them impressive, are found along the Sacred Way.

# Monastiráki

Monastiráki and the Pláka area beyond are wonderful parts of the city, full of historical interest and contemporary diversions. **Monastiráki Square** is named after the monastery founded here in the 17th century, **Panaghía Pantánassa** (currently under restoration). This little monastery has given its name to the metro station whose extension is now open, giving visitors a clear view of the square for the first time in many years. The **flea market**, one of the more over-hyped attractions of the city, is also here. The market proper is in Abyssinia Square, down Ifaístou from Monastiráki Square, but it extends into shops along Ifaístou and the nearby streets, even east up Pandrósou Street to **Mitrópolis Square**. You will find a vast selection of kitsch here, with better-quality goods up Pandrósou. This is a fun, thoroughly vibrant area, particularly on Sundays when Ifaístou is packed.

**Traditional rugs for sale in Monastiráki**

**One of the quiet and attractive streets of Pláka**

## Pláka

The area below the northern slopes of the Acropolis is the **Pláka**, reflecting virtually all the city's past while being very much a part of its present. Cars are banned from many streets and everything here is easily accessible on foot. Pláka has classical, Roman, Byzantine and Ottoman antiquities; restaurants and tavernas; and shops offering jewellery, clothes and a great deal of tourist tat. Although the main thoroughfares are very touristy, a short walk up the hill leads to an area where you can still find attractive, quiet backstreets.

The main commercial street is Adrianoú, the only street that runs through much of Pláka. It extends from the Thesíon metro station, below the lower entrance to the Ancient Greek Agora, all the way past Kydathiníon Street to the 12th-century church of Aghía Aikateríni due east of the Acropolis, almost reaching the Arch of Hadrian. A few blocks from the Ancient Greek Agora the street is interrupted by the still impressive remains of the **Library of Hadrian**, built late in the reign of the Roman emperor Hadrian (AD117–38). Much of this large rectangular building was destroyed, probably in the 3rd century by the Herulian raid. A church was built over the ruins of part of the library early in the 6th century. In the 12th century this church was destroyed and an even smaller church, dedicated to the Virgin Mary, was built. Late in the 19th century the market occupying the site of the Library of Hadrian was burned down along with the church of the Great Virgin Mary. The fire cleared the area for excavations that have progressed off and on ever since.

On the edge of the Library of Hadrian site, and across the street from Monastiráki metro station, is the smaller of the only two mosques left standing hereabouts from the period of the Ottoman occupation. It was built on a high platform in 1759 by the Ottoman governor of Athens, Mustafa Agha Tzisdarakis. The building has been restored and an internal balcony installed to house a folk ceramics collection (open Wed–Mon 9am–2.30pm; admission fee).

The **Roman Agora** (open daily 8am–7pm; admission fee) is just south of Hadrian's Library, up Áreos, left on Dexípou and then right past the church of Ághii Taxiárhi (the Archangels). The area is known as the Roman Agora because most of the excavated remains date to the Roman period, but this area had been used as the commercial centre for Athens since the earliest times. What is now referred to as the Ancient Greek Agora was the civic centre for offices, law courts and temples.

**A Pláka street sign**

The monumental **Gate of Athena Archegetis** (Athena the Leader) consists of four Doric columns supporting an architrave and pediment. This was the entrance to the Roman Agora, paid for by Julius Caesar and Augustus, a huge (111 x 98-m/364 x 322-ft) rectangular court surrounded by columns, behind which were shops. Parts of many of the columns have be re-erected, particularly in the southeast corner of the colonnade, so you can easily see the extent of the building.

Just inside the Roman Agora at the corner of Pános and Pelopídha streets is the **Fethiye Mosque**, the Mosque of the Conquest, constructed over the ruins of an Early Christian basilica shortly after the Ottomans occupied Athens in 1456. It is named after Sultan Mehmet II who captured Constantinople in 1453. The building is not open to the public.

In the 18th century the Tower of the Winds was used as a religious lodge, *tekke*, by a community of Mevlevi dervishes, the famous whirling dervishes, who based their order on the teachings of the 13th century Sufi mystic, Jalal al-Din Rumi.

From the mosque you can easily see the nearby **Tower of the Winds**, known to archaeologists as the Clock of Andronikos Kyrrestos (Kyrros is a town in Syria). This octagonal building, erected in the middle of the first century BC, is famous for its relief carvings of the winged personifications of the winds. A weathervane on top of the building pointed to the appropriate relief as the wind blew. There were sundials on each of the eight sides, and inside was an intricate water-driven 24-hr clock.

The remains of a rectangular building in front of the Tower of the Winds adjacent to Pelopídha are the public latrines built by the Roman emperor Vespasian (AD70–77). The stone slab toilet seats can easily be seen. Continuously running water flushed the waste down to the city's main sewer.

Facing the Tower of the Winds to the north is the ornate entrance gate of an **Islamic school** founded in 1721. Towards the end of the Ottoman period the buildings were used as a prison and condemned prisoners were hanged from a large plane tree in the courtyard. When the new Greek government arrived it carried on the same practice,

**The Tower of the Winds**

confirming the school's evil reputation. The prison was closed in 1911.

By the Islamic school on the left as you walk up the slight incline is the **Museum of Greek Popular Musical Instruments** (open Tues–Sun 10am–2pm, Wed noon–6pm; free), a collection of instruments from all over the country. The exemplary displays contain everything from the *bouzoúki* (a long-necked lute) to the *tsamboúna* (an island bagpipe).

## Adrianoú

Most of Adrianoú is traffic-free and this long, curving street offers a pleasant walk past shops of every description. After crossing Kydatheníon, you end up by a sunken courtyard containing two Ionic columns built during the Roman period. The late 11th-century church of **Aghía Aikateríni**, built on the site of a much earlier, perhaps 5th-century, basilica, is to the left in the courtyard. The church, originally dedicated to St Theodore, was destroyed early in the Ottoman period and abandoned. In 1767 it was acquired by the monastery of St Catherine on Mt Sinai and rebuilt under a new name. The church was enlarged in 1927.

If you look down Lysikrátous Street just left of the church of Aghía Ekateríni you will see the Arch of Hadrian, built in AD132. To the right is the last of the major archaeological monuments standing in Pláka, the **Monument of Lysikrates**, in a small, pleasant square. The monument has survived because it was incorporated into a Capuchin monastery in 1669. In the 19th century it was used as a small library and reading room, frequented by both the French writer Chateaubriand and the English poet Byron when they were visiting Athens. An inscription on the architrave reports that the monument was built by Lysikrates in 335BC.

**Statue of Plato outside the Academy of Athens**

The bases for nine other such monuments have been found in the square and another eight were excavated along Tripódon Street. These monuments were built to celebrate victory in the annual drama contests in honour of the god Dionysos at his theatre on the southeast slope of the Acropolis. All of the 10 Attic tribes entered one chorus of men and one chorus of boys and the victorious chorus was awarded a bronze tripod. Lysikrates proudly displayed the tripod on top of the carved floral arrangement on the conical roof.

Kydatheníon is the second main commercial street in Pláka, running from Filellínon towards the southern slopes of the Acropolis. Number 11 Kydathenion is a fine 19th-century house, of which there are far too many examples throughout Pláka to list here. Across the street is the church of the **Soteíra tou Kottáki**, dedicated to the Virgin Mary and built in the late 11th or early 12th century. It was rebuilt and enlarged in 1908, leaving the original church at the eastern end of the present structure.

At 17 Kydathenion is a museum highlighting an area of Greek culture sometimes ignored by tourists, the **Museum of Greek Folk Art** (open Tues–Sun 9am–2.30pm; admission fee). The fantastic *yéros* costumes worn at carnival time on the island of Skýros on the mezzanine and the paintings by the talented 'primitive' painter Theofilos Hadjimichael (1868–1934) on the first floor are particularly interesting.

Exárhia is the area between Lykavitós *(see page 47)* and the National Archaeological Museum *(see page 48).* In its previous incarnation, this was the centre of Athenian counter-culture (due to its proximity to the university), but is now known for its many bars and restaurants.

## Neoclassical Athens

Perhaps the most impressive neoclassical buildings in the city are the so-called Trilogy of the Academy, University and National Library, all found next to each other along Panepistimíou. The Academy and National Library were designed by the Danish architect Theophil Hansen, and the University by his elder brother Christian. The University was finished by 1842, but the other two were not completed until 1891. The buildings, inspired by the classical architecture of the city, are colourfully painted, giving an idea of how the ancient monuments might originally have looked.

## Downtown Shopping Area

The downtown shopping area is the commercial triangle enclosed by Athinás, Ermoú and Stadíou streets connecting Monastiráki, Omónia and Sýntagma squares. Vehicles are forbidden in most of this area, which has become, in effect, a large shopping district, with trees and benches. Street vendors selling *kouloúria*, the large bread rings, are plentiful, as are many more vendors selling shirts, socks, kitchen appliances, and a varying assortment of other wonders, usually around the church of Ághii Theódori on Evripídou Street, up just a couple of blocks from the central food market.

➤ The huge cast-iron **central food market** is a marvellous place, full of stalls selling fresh meat and fish. It is between Athinás and Aiólou streets, half way between Monastiráki and Omónia squares. Across the road is the fruit-and-vegetable market, and close by are a number of traditional eateries.

**The church of Kapnikaréa in the main shopping district**

## Sýntagma Square

Sýntagma (Constitution) Square is grand and central, with many bank, airline and other major business offices. The northeast metro line starts here, and you can also change to the other two metro lines. The grand old lady of Athenian hotels, the Grande Bretagne is here, and so is the American Express office, one flight up

**The Záppio**

at 2 Ermoú Street on the west side of the square. The pavement cafés here are traditional ports of call, and there is a large post office at the corner of Mitropóleos Street.

## The National Garden, Záppio and Stadium

The large expanse of green southeast of Sýntagma Square and the Parliament building is the **National Garden**, shaded and cool on even the hottest day. The **Záppio**, named after the Zappas brothers who paid for its construction in the late 19th century, is a large exhibition hall and sometime conference centre just south of the National Garden.

The **Stadium** across from the southern curve of the Záppio park is a reconstruction of the ancient stadium first built in 330BC for the athletic events held every four years as part of the Greater Panathenaia. The stadium was completely remodelled by Herodes Atticus for the Panathenaic Festival of AD143–44, providing seating for 50,000 people. Very little of this stadium remained in the 19th century when it was rebuilt, again at the expense of a private Athenian citizen, Yeorgios Averoff, in time to be used for the first modern Olympic Games in 1896.

## Kolonáki

The posh area in town is on the slopes of Lykavitós, a few blocks northwest of Sýntagma Square. The central square here is officially named the Square of the Friendly Society (Platía Filikís Etairías) but always called **Platía Kolonáki**, after the little column few notice under the trees on the southwest side of the square. Many businesses are based here, but what catches the eye is the predominance of fashionable shops and boutiques. The several pavement cafés on two sides of the square are favourite haunts of the Athenian idle rich.

There are two fine museums in Kolonáki. The first of these is the **Goulandris Museum of Cycladic Art** (open Mon, Wed–Fri 10am–4pm, Sun 10am–3pm, closed Tues, Sat; admission fee) on Neofítou Dhoúka Street. The ground floor houses a small gift shop with high-quality reproductions, books and cards, and there is also a garden café. The first floor is devoted to Cycladic artefacts; the second floor covers Greek art from 2000BC to the 4th century AD. The third floor houses temporary exhibitions, while the fourth displays artefacts from the 4th century BC to the 6th century AD, as well as fragments of Cycladic figures from the Keros hoard.

**A Cycladic figurine**

The building is connected to the Helen Strathou neo-classical house, which gives an idea of what life was like for those living in these graceful Kolonáki mansions.

**Benáki Museum** (open Mon, Wed, Fri, Sat 9am–5pm, Thur 9am–midnight, Sun 9am–3pm; admission fee) is on Koubári Street, two blocks closer to Sýntagma Square.

This fabulous collection was established in 1930 by aristocrat and philanthropist Anthony Benakis. Among the most impressive displays are the collections of traditional costumes, mostly bridal and festival dresses, and the reconstructed reception rooms of a mid-18th century Kozáni mansion. Also of great interest are the displays of gold on the ground floor, and the collections relating to the Greek struggle for independence. The museum also has a lovely rooftop café and restaurant.

**A chic Kolonáki café**

## Lykavitós

Behind Kolonáki, **Mt Lykavitós** rises 278m (912ft) above sea level – higher than the Acropolis. A clear path starts from the St George Lycabettus Hotel and a road starting on the northeastern curve goes up most of the way. A *téléférique* going all the way up to the top operates from Ploutárhou, on the mountain's southeastern side (daily 9.30am–4.40pm). If you are blessed with a clear day, the view from the top of Lykavitós is incomparable, including much of Athens and Piraeus, and extending past Aegina down to Ýdra in the Argo-Saronic Gulf. The small church on the summit dedicated to St George may have been built on the site of a Byzantine church dedicated to Profítis Elías. What the restaurant really offers is the view.

## The Archaeological Museum

Galleries in the National Archaeological Museum provide a fascinating tour through ancient Greek art, from the Cycladic Period (3000–2000BC) down to the Roman Period (1st and 2nd centuries AD). Fabulous though the exhibits are, the museum itself has long looked lacklustre and tired, and in October 2000 it was closed for basic repairs and renovation. It will reopen in April 2004.

**The view from Lykavitós**

Some of the galleries had already been renovated before the closure and hopefully provide a clue to how the museum will look when it reopens. The new Egyptian rooms (40 and 41) are beautifully displayed. Also equally well laid out is the Stathatos Collection of gold in the adjoining gallery. Donated in 1971 by Helen Stathatos, this contains items from a large span of Greek history, from Cycladic and Mycenean pieces to Roman and Byzantine works.

Highlights of the museum's collection include: a wonderful bronze statue of Poseidon (*circa* 450BC) that was found in the sea off the island of Évvia; stunning Mycenean gold, much of it from the grave circles at Mycenae in the Peloponnese, excavated by Heinrich Schliemann; and perhaps some of the most prized possessions, the 2nd millennium BC frescoes from Akrotíri on the Cycladic island of Santoríni.

# South of the Acropolis

Situated on Amalías Avenue just south of the Záppio, the huge **Temple of Olympian Zeus** (open daily 8am–7pm; admission fee) is the largest temple to Zeus ever built. It was first planned in 515BC but only completed by the Roman emperor Hadrian in AD132. Of the original 104 colums, only 13 survive today, most of them in a single cluster in one corner of the site.

Between the temple and Pláka is the large and well-preserved **Hadrian's Gate**, through which Hadrian probably marched in triumph to dedicate the temple in AD132. The gate separated the Greek and Roman cities. An inscription on the west side of the gate says, 'This is Athens, the ancient city of Theseus.' On the east side the inscription reads, 'This is the city of Hadrian, not of Theseus.'

There are extensive Roman remains to the south of the temple and evidence of much Roman construction has been identified below ground on the east side of Vasilíssis Ólgas.

Southeast of the Acropolis and almost on a level with it on the Hill of the Muses is the **Philopappos Monument**. It is not within any archaeological site and can be reached at any time. It commands a wonderful view of the Acropolis.

This monument was built as a tomb for Philopappos, the last pretender to the throne of Commagene, a small kingdom in Asia Minor that existed from 80BC until AD72, when it was made part

**A classical relief in the Archaeological Museum**

of the Roman Empire. Philopappos settled in Athens and became a benefactor of the city, for which the citizens awarded him with this tomb dated between AD114 and 116.

Scattered remains of a **Sanctuary to Dionysos** (open daily 8am–7pm; admission fee) are just inside the entrance to the archaeological site, but you will be drawn to the **Theatre of Dionysos**, built in approximately 330BC to seat 15,000 people. The front row had 67 thrones; the one in the centre was for the high priest of Dionysos.

The wonderful **Odeion of Herodes Atticus** right below the Acropolis was built by Herodes Atticus in AD174. It seats 5,000 people and the original structure was roofed in cedar. It was reconstructed, without a roof, in 1858 and is now used for concerts and plays in association with the Festival of Athens. It is a beautiful setting, but the seats are hard and there are no backrests.

**The Temple of Olympian Zeus by night**

## Outside Athens

The beautiful **Kaisarianí Monastery** (open Tues–Sun
8.30am–3pm; admission fee), 16km (10 miles) from central
Athens on the slopes of Mt Hymettos, was founded in the 11th
century and prospered in the 12th and 13th centuries. When the
Turks occupied Athens in 1458, the bishop of Kaisarianí was
chosen to present the keys of the city to Sultan Mehmet II, who
thereupon exempted the monastery from taxation. After
independence, however, it was unable to maintain itself and
was gradually abandoned. The frescoes in the church date to
the period of Turkish occupation.

The mosaics in the **Dafní Monastery** (temporarily closed)
are masterpieces of Byzantine art, dating from approximately
1100. The other two roughly contemporary survivors of this
quality of mosaics are in the Monastery of Ísios Loukás, near
Delphi, and Néa Moní on the island of Híos.

The ancient site of Eleusis is in the modern town of Elefsí-
na, west of Dafní. **Ancient Eleusis** (open Tues–Sun 8.30am–
3pm; admission fee, except Sun, when it is free) was an independent city founded in the 15th century BC that came to
be associated with the story of Demeter and Persephone
described in the 7th-century BC Homeric *Hymn to Demeter*.

## Piraeus

Southeast of Athens along the coast is the port of **Piraeus**, a
city very much in its own right although you won't be able to
tell precisely where Athens ends and Piraeus begins.
Many ferries, for instance those to Crete and the hydrofoil
to Aegina, leave from the main harbour in front of the metro
station; if you are going on to one of the other Aegean
Islands it is possible that your ship will leave from either the
**Pasalimáni** or **Zéa harbours** on the other side of the city.
You might well come down here for any one of the many
fish *tavérnes* found in the little harbour of **Mikrolímano**. A

**Piraeus Harbour**

visit to the **Archaeological Museum** (open Tues–Sun 8.30am–3pm; admission fee), with its superb collection of ancient bronzes, is also highly recommended.

After the large yacht harbour of **Kalamáki** is a well-organised public beach at **Ághios Kosmás**. **Glyfádha** is a busy and pleasant seaside suburb with a yacht harbour, a good public beach and many restaurants, notably on the street running away from the sea to the main square. **Voúla**, further southeast, has another good public beach. The major resort area of **Vouliagméni** has two good public beaches and several hotels, notably the luxury hotel Astir Palace.

## ANCIENT SITES IN ATTICA

### Sounion

**Cape Sounion**, the southernmost point of Attica, easily reached by public transport, is the site of the 5th century BC marble **Temple of Poseidon** (open daily 10am–sunset; admission fee). Its history parallels that of the Parthenon in Athens in that work on a temple began here after the defeat of the Persians at Marathon in 490BC and the Persians destroyed this temple in 480BC before it was completed. The Greek vow not to rebuild the temples and shrines destroyed by the Persians lasted here for 36 years; the classical temple we see today was built from 444–440BC.

## Marathon

The battle of **Marathon** in 490BC was fought on a plain by the sea 42km (26 miles) northeast of Athens, between the villages of Néa Mákri and Marathóna. What can be seen today associated with the battle are the burial mound of the Athenians, the burial mound identified by the excavator as that of the Plataians, and the **Archaeological Museum** (all open Tues–Sun 8.30am–3pm; admission fee).

The **burial mound of the Athenians**, simply a circular mound of earth 9m (30ft) high, 50m (164ft) in diameter, and 185m (600ft) in circumference, has a modern copy of the ancient stele on the top (the original is in the National Archaeological Museum). The mound is impressive, but nothing compared to the victory it symbolises. The mighty Persian empire, the largest on earth, had sent its army against Athens, and approximately 9,000 Athenian soldiers were

**Temple of Poseidon at Sounion**

joined before the battle by 1,000 soldiers from Plataea, a town in Boeotia. A runner was sent to ask the Spartans for help, but the Spartans only arrived after the battle. The Athenians won against overwhelming odds, with the Persians losing 6,400 men and the Athenians 192. The Athenians were cremated and buried together in the mound. The **mound of the Plataeans** is near the archaeological museum, about 3km (2 miles) to the west. There is nothing to mark the Persian graves, but they seem to have been buried to the northeast, in the area around the small church of the Panaghía Mesosporítissa.

## Brauron, Rhamnous and Amphiareion

Ancient **Brauron** (open Fri, Sat, Sun 8.30am–3pm; admission fee), dedicated to the goddess Artemis, is between Pórto Ráfti and Loútsa on the east coast of Attica 38km (22 miles) from central Athens. The sanctuary of Brauron was founded in the 6th century BC and became prosperous in the late 6th and early 5th centuries BC. Artemis was worshipped here as the goddess of hunting and vegetation, and part of her important quadrilennial ceremonies involved young girls dressed as bears propitiating the goddess. There also is a small **museum** (open Tues–Sun 8.30am–3pm; admission fee).

**Rhamnous** (open daily 8am–6pm; admission fee), the site of an ancient fortress town on the northern borders of Attica with a sanctuary of Nemesis, is 53km (33 miles) from Athens. The sanctuary contains two **temples**. The older, built right after 490BC, was dedicated to Nemesis and also to Themis, the god of justice. The slightly larger Doric temple of Nemesis, built in 436–432BC, almost touches the older temple. The **garrison town**, roughly 800m (half a mile) down from the sanctuary on the shore, flourished in the 5th and 4th centuries BC.

The city-state that built the **Sanctuary of Amphiareion** (open Tues–Sun 8.30am–3pm; admission fee) late in the 5th century BC was ancient Oropos, now buried beneath the modern town of Skála Oropós, where the ferry leaves for Euboia (Évvia). The sanctuary was particularly well known in the Hellenistic period, visited by people from all over the Greek world in search of advice or medical help. The suppliant sacrificed a ram to Amphiaraos, after which a dream would either cure the illness or answer a question.

## The Origin of the Marathon

Our modern word 'marathon' seems to be based upon a doubtful interpretation. The story is, of course, that after the battle a man named Pheidippides ran the approximately 26 miles to Athens to proclaim the victory and then promptly died of exhaustion. However, this version seems to have come from Plutarch, writing 530 years after the event.

Herodotus, who was alive in 490BC and later collected reports from men who fought in the battle, reported an entirely different and far more interesting tale. He wrote that Pheidippides ran not from Marathon to Athens but from Athens to Sparta, and before, not after the battle. Herodotus does not say that Pheidippides was any the worse for his effort. He ran the 246km (153 miles) to solicit help from the Spartans against the impending Persian attack. The Spartans delayed, claiming that they had to observe a religious festival, and arrived three days after the battle.

Herodotus reported that, while he was running, Pheidippides was visited by the god Pan, who complained that the Athenians did not give him honour. Pheidippides apparently made the correct response, for when the battle came Pan is supposed to have struck terror into the hearts of the attacking Persians, the origin of our word 'panic'. The appearance of Pan to Pheidippides is explained by the fact that many long-distance runners often suffer hallucinations while running. Certainly, after the battle there appear shrines to Pan all over Attica where there had been none before.

# CENTRAL GREECE

## To the East

After **Kaména Voúrla** on the National Road, just before the turning for Ámfissa and Delphi up over Mt Parnassós, a large, unattractive modern statue of an ancient Spartan warrior marks the site of **Thermopylae**. Here the Spartan king, Leonidas, held the then narrow pass against the much larger attacking Persian army in 480BC until a Greek traitor showed the Persians a mountain path leading behind the Spartan line. All but one of the 300 Spartan defenders were killed. The monument erected in their honour included the message to their city, 'Go, stranger, and tell the Lacedaemonians (Spartans) that here we lie, obedient to their commands'.

In antiquity the small port city of **Vólos** was Iolkos, the city from which Jason and his Argonauts set off to find the

**A beach on the Pílion Peninsula**

Golden Fleece along the shores of the Black Sea. Today there is little to see except a small but good **archaeological museum** (open Tues–Sun 8.30am–3pm; admission fee).

Fruits in honey, a Pílion speciality

**Mt Pílion**, the mythological home of the centaurs, is a beautiful mountainous peninsula ending in a curve to the southwest. Because it was far from the Ottoman authorities it developed as a centre of Greek culture in the 17th and 18th centuries. It is dotted, particularly in the northeast, with very pretty villages: **Makrinítsa**; the larger **Zagóra**, famous for its apple crop; the popular summer resort of **Ághios Ioánnis**, **Mylopótamos**, **Miliés**, **Vyzítsa** and small beaches. The entire peninsula is well worth exploration, but it can be crowded in the high summer season.

North of Lárisa is the narrow pass between Mt Óssa and Mt Ólympos, the **Vale of Témpi**, the gateway between northern and southern Greece. The Piniós River runs through the gorge, and here Daphne, the mythological daughter of the river god, was pursued by Apollo. Daphne called for help to her father, who turned her into a tree, forever chaste. That there are many laurel trees here is fitting, for the Greek *dáfni* is laurel in English.

The green passage with its lovely river is a rest stop for truckers and tourists, who pause here to eat at the roadside restaurants and perhaps visit the small church of Aghía Paraskeví, reached by crossing a small suspension bridge over the river.

## Metéora

Considerably further up the Piniós River, just north of the town of Kalambáka, is **Metéora**, where an astonishing group of rock towers is home to more monasteries than anywhere else in Greece except Mt Áthos. Metéora means 'suspended in the air', which these monasteries certainly seem to be. The area has served as a holy retreat since at least the 10th century, but the first monastery (Doupianí) was built in the 11th century. In the 15th and 16th centuries there were 24.

**Looking out across the rock spires of Metéora**

The largest is **Megálou Meteórou** (open Wed–Mon 10am–5pm), established in 1344. The second largest, **Varlám** (open Fri–Wed 9am–2pm and 3.15–5pm), was established at approximately the same time, but the monastery buildings were constructed in the middle of the 15th century. **Roussánou** (open 9am–6pm), the most dramatically located and frequently photographed, was established by monks in the mid-16th century but is now run by nuns. **Aghías Triádhos** (open Fri–Wed 9am–12.30pm and 3–5pm) was built in the third quarter of the 15th century. **Aghíou Stefánou** (open Tues–Sun 9am–2pm and 3.30–6pm), also now a convent, was established at the end of the 14th century. **Aghíou Nikoláou** (open Sat–Thur 9am–3.30pm) was founded *circa* 1527.

# Delphi

On the way to Delphi, make the short detour after the market town of **Levadiá** to visit the large 10th-century **Ísios Loukás Monastery**. The serene monastery looks down over a quiet valley and it has some fine mosaics and wall paintings.

The archaeological site of **Delphi** (open daily 7.30am–6.45pm; admission fee) lies on the slopes of **Mt Parnassós** along the route connecting the plains of Boeotia to the east with the Corinthian Gulf ports in the west, at an ancient crossroads. The area has been sacred to Apollo since great antiquity. Here the god's voice was said to be heard through the oracle. The oracle was of great significance in the Greek world from the 8th century BC, ending only in the 4th century AD.

> The Delphic oracle was called the Pythia, a woman who spoke in a trance once a month and whose words were translated by the sanctuary's priests in answer to supplicants' questions.

Approaching the site from **Aráhova**, on the right is the **Castalian Spring**. The fountain nearest the road was in use from mid-6th century BC until late Hellenistic or early Roman times, when it was replaced by another deeper in the cleft and cut from the mountainside.

To the left are the **Athena Pronaia Sanctuary** and the Gymnasium Complex. Athena Pronaia means 'Athena before the temple' and refers to the sanctuary being on the way ancient visitors would go as they approached the Apollo Sanctuary. Some columns from the second Athena Pronaia Temple are still standing, but the most interesting and beautiful structure here is the 4th-century BC **Tholos**, a circular building made of black and white marble. Archaeologists still do not know what it was used for. The **Gymnasium Complex** had both covered and open tracks and baths, including a very well-preserved circular pool from the classical period.

**The Tholos in the Sanctuary of Athena Pronaia**

The path from the entrance to the **Apollo Sanctuary** is lined with monuments and treasuries and stoas all the way up to the dominant Temple of Apollo. Perhaps the most interesting is the **Athenian Stoa**, which displayed the extremely thick cables the Persians had used to hold their ships together when forming the pontoon bridge they used to cross the Hellespont. The remains of the **Temple of Apollo** visible on the site are from the 4th century BC.

The **theatre** above the Apollo Temple was built in the 3rd and 2nd centuries BC, and could seat 5,000 people. Its acoustics are impressive and it has a wonderful view over the site and across the valley. The well preserved **stadium** is up through the trees, its polygonal retaining wall from the 5th century BC. Starting and finishing lines are cut into stone at either end.

The **Delphi Museum** (open Tues–Sun 7.30am–6.45pm, Mon noon–6.45pm; admission fee) has finds from the sanctuaries and the ancient town, all well displayed. In the vestibule is a large carved Roman marble ball, the *ómphalos*, or navel, symbolising Delphi as being the centre of the world. We will mention here only some of the displays in the several galleries on the upper floor. The **silver bull** is the largest surviving precious metal sculpture from antiquity. It dates from the 6th century BC and may have been a gift from King Croesus. The full height of the 6th-century BC **Naxian Sphinx** was 11.5m (38ft). The **Siphnian Treasury friezes** in the same room depict the Trojan War, the battle between the gods and the giants, and the judgement of Paris. The Apollo Gallery has the **statue of Apollo** from the 4th-century BC temple. The **Charioteer Gallery** has the best-known statue in Delphi by far, the hollow bronze statue of a charioteer, made in approximately 470BC.

## Northern Coast of the Gulf of Corinth

**Itéa**, the port town below Delphi, is memorable primarily for all its bauxite mounds, but **Galaxídhi** – a prosperous shipping town in the 18th and 19th centuries – is a beautiful little harbour town. There are many pleasant restaurants and bars along the waterfront.

**Náfpaktos** is situated further along the coast to the west. The tiny port in what is now a sprawling town was vitally important to medieval sea power. Cervantes, author of *Don Quixote*, fought and lost an arm in the Battle of Lepanto here in 1517, a sea battle in which a combined Spanish, Venetian and papal fleet destroyed the Ottoman navy.

**The Gulf of Corinth as seen from Náfpaktos**

# IONIAN SEA COAST – EPIRUS

The city of **Messolóngi** is famous because Lord Byron died here in 1824 and because the second Ottoman siege of the city during the War of Independence ended dramatically and bloodily for the Greeks in 1826. Other than its historical associations, however, Messolóngi is drab.

If you are driving to Árta or Ioánnina, stay on the heavily travelled main road that passes through Agrínio. If you are driving to Lefkáda, Préveza, Párga or Corfu, turn left just north of Messolóngi and pass through Aitolikó and Astakós.

## Messolóngi

During the War of Independence Messolóngi was a centre of the fractious Greek forces, but as a garrison town it was badly defended, with only a hastily erected earthen wall 1.5m (5ft) high. It was besieged twice by Ottoman forces. The first siege lasted from the autumn of 1822 until the spring of 1823. Despite far superior numbers, Ottoman army incompetence enabled the Greeks to repulse attacks and eventually turn the tide, routing and killing many of the besiegers.

The second Ottoman siege of Messolóngi was a completely different affair. The city was completely surrounded in the summer of 1825. Some Greek ships managed to bring supplies through the Ottoman naval blockade, but in November the Egyptian army under Ibrahim Pasha came to help the Turks. In the spring of 1826 attacks were increased, and by April the town was near starvation. About 7,000 of the town's inhabitants decided to break through the besieging forces, rushing out en masse. Most didn't make it through the Ottoman lines, and many of those who did were caught and killed in the mountains. Approximately 2,000 people who had remained in the town were killed when the Turks entered the next day. Only about 1,500 Greeks survived. Messolóngi itself was left burned and lifeless.

This road runs by the sea most of the way, until Páleros, and provides wonderful views over the water towards Itháki and Lefkáda. Don't do this at night, however. The road has no lighting, there are occasional potholes, and sometimes free-ranging cows and donkeys wander onto it.

The entrance to the **Amvrakikós Gulf** is the western border of **Epirus**, Greece's northern corner, that extends up to the Albanian border. There is a small airport at **Áktion** (Latin Actium), on the southern side of the entrance to the gulf. In 31BC Mark Antony camped here, thereby provid-

**A gate in the walls of Roman Nikópolis**

ing the name for the naval battle fought off the coast in which Octavian (later Augustus) ended any hopes Mark Antony and Cleopatra had of ruling the Roman Empire. The small fort by the sea that you may notice on the southern side of the entrance before entering the tunnel is Venetian, as is the much larger fort on the northern side of the entrance.

Octavian, however, built his victory city, **Nikópolis**, 5km (3 miles) north of Préveza. The modern road cuts right through the Roman city walls, with their three distinctive bands of brick. Inside these walls on the western side of the road is the Early Christian basilica of **Ághios Alkýsonos**, of which the square portal is well preserved. The Roman

**Odeum** is on the eastern side of the road. This small theatre is in much better condition than the large Roman theatre nearby. The entrance to the small **Archaeological Museum**, near the sign pointing to Mítikas, is not clearly marked.

**Kassópi**, the 4th-century BC capital of the Kassopaian tribe, was built on a bowl of a plateau above mosquito-infested marshland and commanded fine views over the Ionian Sea and the Amvrakikós Gulf. The city had about 9,000 inhabitants at its most prosperous.

Roughly 300m (330yds) to the east is the 16th-century **Zálongo Monastery**, at the foot of cliffs beneath the towering cement statue of women holding hands and dancing. This statue commemorates the desperate end of the 15-year resistance by people from the area of Soúli against Ali Pasha, the brutal ruler based in Ioánnina. Ali Pasha's troops besieged the Souliots throughout the summer of 1803 until, without water, they signed a formal surrender and guarantee of their safety. About 2,000 Souliots headed for Párga and 1,000 headed for Préveza. Ali Pasha attacked both groups. Those going to Párga managed to reach their destination, but the 1,000 Souliots trying to reach Préveza were massacred in the monastery. About 60 women and children fled up the mountain. When they reached the top the women threw their children over the cliff and then, dancing traditional Souliot dances, jumped over the edge themselves.

The **Nekromantíon**, the ancient Oracle of the Dead, is by the village of **Mesopótamos** on a small hill. Most of the remains here date from the 3rd or 4th centuries BC, and the small church on top of the ruins was built in the 18th century. The large polygonal wall on the way to the underground chamber and the chamber itself are of much greater antiquity. This may have been where Homer tells us Odysseus came to visit Hades and, according to Herodotus, where Periandros, the tyrant of Corinth, came to communicate with his dead wife.

The **River Ahéron** meanders through the plain here before entering the Ionian Sea at Mesopótamos. This surprisingly narrow, deep and fast running stream was supposed to be one of the entrances to Hades.

## Árta

**Árta** was the capital city of the Despotate of Epirus, one of the four despotates into which the Byzantine Empire splintered when the Fourth Crusade occupied Constantinople in 1204. Although the site dates back to ancient times, Árta's most impressive remains are medieval. Much of the Byzantine castle remains, and there are four 13th-century churches and one 14th-century church, most of them near the castle walls. The two sites not be missed in Árta are the stone bridge parallel to the modern bridge on the northern side of the city and the despotates' cathedral church.

**The stone bridge at Árta**

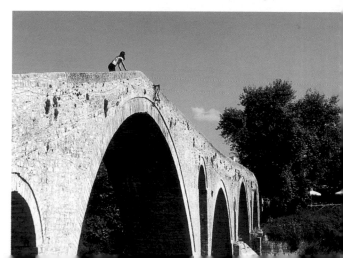

The **bridge** has foundations dating from the Hellenistic period, but what you see today was built in the first decade of the 16th century. As with many bridges in southeastern Europe, there is a legend that the bridge kept falling down until the master builder entombed his wife, alive, inside the foundations.

The church of the **Panaghía Parigorítissa** (Virgin Mary the Consoler), built in 1285, looks like a very large, plain Byzantine box as you approach, but the interior is extraordinary. The central dome, 23m (70ft) high, is supported by three upper levels of cantilevered columns and is decorated with a mosaic of Christ Pantokrátor (Universal Ruler).

Árta's lively market has excellent produce

## Párga

**Párga** is a pretty medieval port town with a Venetian castle dating from 1624. The French under Napoleon protected the city from Ali Pasha, but when the British became the protecting power they eventually, in 1819, turned the city over to him. The people of Párga all moved to Corfu, leaving Ali Pasha with an empty city. The fish restaurants and shops along the quay are attractive and a lovely place to sit in spring, but in the summer months Párga is packed.

## Ioánnina

Invading Bulgars, Slavs, Normans, Serbs, Albanians and Turks all challenged Byzantine rule in **Ioánnina**, successfully on many occasions. The Ottomans captured the city in 1430 and Turkish rule ended only 483 years later, in 1913. Until the late 16th century, the Ottoman Empire was a growing force, the provider in many ways of a tolerant, stable government. This was followed by a long period of decline, particularly in the 18th and 19th centuries, when the empire's subjects longed to be free of what had become arbitrary and corrupt rule. In Ioánnina the dominant figure in this context was Ali Pasha, who ruled much of western Greece from 1788 until 1822. Ali Pasha was brutal, extremely so, but his stable government enabled the area to prosper.

The **kástro**, the walled area on the peninsula jutting into Lake Pamvótis, is the obvious focus for any visitor. Inside the walls are the quiet streets and small houses of the old city. The **Old Synagogue**, which may have first been built in the 10th century, is also here, on Justinian Street. The Romaniot (meaning indigenous Greek Jews, not Sephardic Jews from the Iberian peninsula) Jewish community in Ioánnina now numbers only approximately 70 people. The 16th-century New Synagogue was destroyed by the occupying German forces during World War II.

Signs for the **Municipal Museum** (open Thur–Tues, Apr–Sept 9am–1.30pm and 3.30–8pm; Oct–Mar 9am–1.30pm and 3.30–6.30pm; admission fee) lead to the

Ioánnina's kástro, with its minaret

early 17th-century **Aslan Pasha Mosque** in the northwestern corner of the peninsula. Most of the items on display are from the Greek War of Independence and the 1913 campaign, which finally drove the Turks from Epirus.

Ali Pasha had the **Fetiye Mosque** built in the southeastern corner of the kástro. Outside the mosque are two unmarked graves, one containing the remains of Ali Pasha's first wife, Esmine, and the other containing the headless remains of Ali Pasha himself. When Ottoman forces finally killed him in

---

### The 'Lion of Ioannina'

Ali Pasha was born in Tepeleni in southern Albania sometime in the early 1740s. He became the leader of a band of brigands and then served with several Ottoman leaders, eventually becoming pasha first of Trikkala and then Ioannina in 1788 through intrigue and murder. His Albanian followers, known as Skipetars, were the core of his military strength, and he was skilled at playing off different factions against each other; he was also brutal. At the height of his powers he ruled over a large area of Albania and northern and central Greece.

The positive side of Ali Pasha's rule was that the stability he imposed enabled the territory to flourish. He financed Greek schools and many of the Greeks he employed later became prominent participants in the Greek War of Independence.

In 1820 Ali Pasha tried to have one of his enemies in the sultan's court poisoned. When the plot was discovered the Ottoman army was sent to surround Ioánnina. Ali Pasha fled to the island in Lake Pamvótis after months of siege. On 5 February 1822 Greek bodyguards were unable to prevent attacking Turks from killing Ali Pasha by firing up through the floorboards of the monastery guesthouse. Ali Pasha's head was carried on a platter throughout the area for three days and then sent to the sultan, who had it placed outside the palace on a pike. Months later the Albanians in Istanbul received permission to bury the head.

1822, his head was cut off and sent in triumph to the Porte in Istanbul.

The shaded park area outside the kástro down by the waterfront has a few restaurants and there are usually cart peddlers selling sweets, nuts and souvenirs. Boats leave every half hour for the 10-minute ride to the island, once a haven for monasteries. The main path past the

**An Ottoman relief in the kástro**

**fish restaurants** by the boat landing forks to the right towards the monastery of Ághios Nikólaos ton Filanthropínon and to the left towards the monastery of Aghios Panteleimonas. The 16th-century church in the **Ághios Nikólaos ton Filanthropínon Monastery**, near the top of the small hill, has wall paintings in quite good condition. The church is also supposed to be the site of a 'secret school', widely believed in modern Greece to have been needed to protect the Greek language and Orthodox faith from being extinguished by the Ottomans. The fork to the left leads to the **Ághios Pantelímonas Monastery** where Ali Pasha was was killed (*see panel opposite*).

## 1912–1913 War Museum

South of Ioánnina, 27km (17 miles) along the road to Árta, a small sign reads '1912–1913 War Museum', which was the Greek army headquarters during the 1912–13 campaign. This was an extraordinary victory for the Greek attacking troops over the far more numerous Turkish troops defending Ioánnina, involving attacks up the western heights. The battle lasted six weeks and ended on 21 Feb-

ruary 1913, when one contingent of Greek troops got behind the Turkish lines. This Greek victory ended 483 years
of Turkish rule in Epirus.

## Dodona

Situated 21km (13 miles) southwest of Ioánnina, in a
beautiful bowl of a valley, is the **Oracle of Zeus** at
**Dodona** (daily 8.30am–5pm; admission fee). This is the
oldest oracle in Greece, older than the Oracle of Apollo in
Delphi, since it was in use from the Early Bronze Age. In
the 12th century BC the Molossians, a Hellenic tribe, settled here after driving the
also Hellenic Thesprotians
towards the south. In the
4th century BC Olympias,
the daughter of the Molossian king, married Philip II
of Macedonia and became
the mother of Alexander
the Great. The most famous
Molossian king was
Pyrrhos (297–71BC), whom
we know for his costly
'Pyrrhic' victory over the
Romans in 279BC. Nonetheless, Pyrrhos's time was a
prosperous one for Epirus, bringing new cities and new
buildings. The restored theatre, which can seat 18,000
people, was built under his reign.

> Dodona's sanctuary was
> surrounded by bronze
> cauldrons set on tripods
> so close together that
> the cauldrons touched.
> When one was struck
> they all vibrated, and
> the sound they pro-
> duced was interpreted.
> Later prophecies were
> made on the basis of the
> rustling leaves of the
> sacred oak tree.

In 168BC, when the Romans finally captured Epirus
they destroyed 70 Epirot cities and carried 150,000 people
away as slaves. Augustus and other Roman emperors supported the sanctuary, which probably continued to operate
until the emperor Theodosius decreed the end of pagan
practices in AD391. The sacred oak was cut down and

uprooted, and Dodona became the seat of a bishop, with a basilica built in the sanctuary in the 5th or 6th century. Gothic invasions, however, made life here untenable, and the inhabitants moved to the new city the emperor Justinian established on the peninsula jutting out into Lake Pamvótis. There are no remains to be found, but apparently Justinian built a church dedicated to St John the Baptist on the peninsula; hence the name Ioánnina.

The theatre at the sanctuary of Dodona

A large limestone **cave**, with the requisite stalactites and stalagmites can be visited in the village of **Pérama** just north of Ioánnina, on the road heading east towards Métsovo. Further north, at the small village of **Kalpáki**, the Greek army stopped the Italian advance in the winter of 1940–41. This was an extraordinary, heroic accomplishment by a small country against its much larger neighbour, and it did wonders for Greek self-respect. Marble busts of the major figures – King George II, the dictator Ioannis Metaxas, and the army commander, Alexandros Papagos – are on the west side of the road. Next to the small **War Museum** (open Tues–Sun 9am–noon and 5–8pm) on the east side of the road is a bust of Mordechai Frizis, a Jewish colonel killed by the Italians during the Greek advance north of the present Albanian border.

## Voidhomátis – Aoós Valley

About 20km (12 miles) north of Kalpáki the road rises for a few miles and then drops down into a beautiful valley in which the Voidomátis and Aoós rivers join after cutting spectacular gorges through the **Píndhos Mountains**. About 200m (650ft) off the road to the right (east), on the south bank of the Voidomátis River, there is a pleasant *tavérna* serving delicious and inexpensive grilled fresh trout and a variety of other dishes. Another 300m (1,000ft) up the dirt road by the river is one of the many arched stone bridges for which Epirus is famous. This one, built in 1853, is beautifully situated among plane trees.

The **Aoós River** breaks from the mountains just south of **Kónitsa** after cutting the spectacular **Víkos Gorge** between **Mt Smólikas** (2,637m/8,650ft), the highest peak in the Píndhos Mountains, and **Mt Gamíla**. The 1870

**The Víkos Gorge in the Píndhos**

arched stone bridge here has a bell beneath the apex of the arch that rings with any strong wind to warn travellers of the danger of being blown off.

## Zagória

The Vikos Gorge is part of **Zagória**, a truly unspoilt region of the Píndhos Mountains known for its dramatic mountain scenery and its timeless stone-built villages. The entrance to the southern route into Zagória is clearly marked 19km (12 miles) north of Ioánnina. The route to **Kípi** has three arched stone 18th- and 19th-century bridges, but more are scattered throughout the area. **Monodhéndri** is a good place to stay because it has a hotel and several guest houses, and here you can begin the wonderful walk through the Vikos Gorge to Pápingo, a 6-hr or longer trek along the valley of the Voidhomátis River.

You can view the gorge from a cliff-side path leading from the 14th-century **Aghía Paraskeví Monastery** down from the village, but take care – there is no retaining barrier. For a safer, although higher, view, drive 7km (4 miles) up the partially paved road above Monodhéndri, past the unusual piles of striated limestone to the end, and then follow the stone path. At places the cliff drops 1,000m (3,000ft) down to the river.

The turn for the northern area of Zagória is 4km (2½ miles) north of Kalpáki. At the village of Arísti the road drops down to cross the very cold water of the Voidhomátis over a narrow stone bridge (1873). This is a park area, with beautiful plane trees and a pleasant riverside walk down to the river-bank *tavérna*. The road then rises through 20 hairpin turns to reach **Megálo Pápingo**, facing the Víkos Gorge between the village and the heights of **Mt Gamíla**. The smaller village of **Mikró Pápingo** is another 4km (2½ miles) further on. The trail (4hrs plus each way) up to the mountain lake **Drakolímni** (Dragon Lake) on the edge of the cliff begins from Megálo Pápingo.

## Métsovo

The mountain town of **Métsovo**, 56km (35 miles) east of Ioánnina over a good but winding mountain road, is Greece's largest Vlach community, the Vlachs being a non-Greek people who settled in Greece in antiquity. Their language is a derivative of Latin, and very close to Romanian. Traditionally they are transhumant shepherds, but many are now settled, and in Métsovo they are thriving, more than any other mountain settlement in Epirus. Métsovo has many hotels and an art gallery, but the most interesting site in town is the **Tosítsa family mansion**, rebuilt and refurbished in the 1950s and now an interesting museum of 19th-century mountain life.

**The attractive streets of Métsovo**

Don't miss the **Aghíou Nikoláou Monastery** below the southern side of town by the Árahthos River. It was founded in the 14th century and rebuilt around 1700. The interior walls and ceilings of the church are covered with wall paintings, providing an exceedingly rare view of how Greek Orthodox churches used to look. Since most members of the congregation couldn't read, biblical stories were painted on the interior walls. These paintings had long been lost, covered with lampblack, and were only restored in 1960.

# MACEDONIA AND THRACE

## Kastoriá

This city on the western shore of Lake Kastoriá in western Macedonia was a small city-state until incorporated into the Macedonian Empire. After Roman rule it was ruled from Constantinople, and the emperor Justinian (526–65) fortified the

**Byzantine frescoes in Kastoriá**

town. The town also saw heavy fighting during both World War II and the ensuing Greek Civil War. There are no more beavers (*kastóri* means beaver in Greek) in the lake, having been exterminated by hunting, but the fur trade that has flourished here since at least the 17th century, under Ottoman rule, continues with imported pelts.

The city has at least 40 Byzantine churches, its main attraction, including: the 12th-century church of **St George at Omorfoklissía** (a few kilometres out-of-town), with 13th-century wall paintings; the church of **St Stephen**, with 9th-10th- and 12th-century wall paintings; and the 10th-century church of the **Panaghía (Holy Virgin) Koumbelidhikí**, with 13th- and 17th-century wall paintings. The **Mavriótissa Monastery** may have been built by Alexios I Komnenos after putting down a revolt in 1084.

The city also has many impressive mansions, built by the wealthy fur traders. A fine early (16th- or 17th-century) example now houses the **Kastoriá Folklore Museum** and an 18th-century mansion contains the **Kastoriá Costume Museum** (both open daily, 10am–noon and 4–6pm; admission fee), both near the lake.

**Brown bear at Nymfío**

## Préspa

The extraordinary wildlife refuge of **Préspa** is some 36km (22 miles) north of Kastoriá, where Greece borders on both Albania and the Former Yugoslav Republic of Macedonia (FYROM). This wonderful high-altitude bowl of a valley holds the two lakes of **Megáli** (Large) and **Mikrí** (Small) **Préspa**, the nesting place for 260 species of birds, including the large Dalmatian and great white pelican. This is an exceptionally large number of species for such a small area. The Society for the Protecton of Prespes operates two information centres, one in **Ághios Yermanós** and one in **Psarádhes**, well worth visiting to get a better understanding of this remarkable habitat.

Préspa also has 14 Byzantine and post-Byzantine churches, the oldest being the **Ághios Ahíllios Basilica** on the island of the same name in Mikrí Préspa. The powerful Bulgarian tsar Samuel had his castle here. Samuel was defeated and killed by the Byzantine emperor Basil II, known as the 'Bulgar Slayer', in 1019, and Samuel's remains may have been kept in an urn in the basilica.

Small boat excursions leave from Psarádhes to visit the abandoned medieval monastic retreats on the shore of Megáli Préspa.

## Édessa and Véria

Édessa, further east, is primarily known for its prodigious waterfall. The area south of the Édessa–Thessaloníki road has several imposing and well displayed **Macedonian**

**tombs** (The Great Tomb, Kinch's Tomb, The Tomb of Lyson and Kallikles; open Tues–Sun 8.30am–3pm; admission fee). Some 4km (2½ miles) south is **Náoussa**, home to the Boutári winery, which produces some of the best wine in Greece and gives tours to visitors. **Aristotle's School** can be seen in the town.

The prosperous agricultural centre of **Véria** has been thriving since antiquity and is a good base for visiting Lefkádia, Vergína and Náoussa. St Paul's visit here is commemorated by a modern monument built on the traditional site where he delivered his sermons. The city has more than 45 Byzantine churches and there are several Ottoman buildings remaining from Turkish rule in Véria between 1433 and 1912.

Much good restoration work has been done here in recent years. Visit the wonderful new **Byzantine Museum** at Thomídhou 26 (open Tues–Sun 8.30am–3pm; admission

## The Bears of Nymfío

The Vlach village of Nymfío, on the eastern flanks of Mt Vermio, has large houses built by successful 19th-century cotton and tobacco traders. It is an unspoilt resort well worth visiting for its natural beauty, but the most interesting thing here is the Brown Bear Sanctuary and Brown Bear Information Centre run by the Arcturos Environmental Centre (tel: 2386 415 000 <www.arcturos.gr>). Here bears that have been rescued from captivity are looked after and released into a 5-hectare (12-acre) enclosure (even a short spell in captivity makes them unfit to survive in the wild). The organisation also runs a similar programme for wolves, based at Agrapidhiá. Arcturos not only rescues bears and wolves, but is a campaigning body that has been instrumental in creating cross-border agreements with other Balkan countries to protect the migration routes of the large mammals that live in the mountains on the Greek/Albanian/Bulgarian border.

**Mosaic of a lion at Pélla**

fee) for basic information about the churches and their locations, and take the interesting walking tour the museum runs daily from here. The restored areas of Kyriótissa and Barboúta, the Jewish quarter by the Tripótomas River provide a wonderful view of 18th- and 19th-century life.

## Vergína and Pélla

The farming village of **Vergína** is the site of the ancient city of **Aigai** (open daily 8am–7pm, Mon noon–7pm; admission fee), inhabited from the Early Bronze Age (3rd millennium BC) to the 2nd century BC when it may have been destroyed by the Romans. Today it is famous for the **royal tombs**, particularly the **tomb of King Philip II of Macedon** (359–36BC), father of Alexander the Great. The wall paintings and precious objects, such as the gold couch, are clearly displayed in an underground hall in the actual excavation of the tomb itself, although the tombs themselves are closed to the public. Two other Macedonian tombs are a short distance to the southeast, towards the **Hellenistic Palace**.

**Pélla** became the capital of Macedonia at the beginning of the 4th century BC, although royal burials continued to be made at Aigai/Vergína. This was the capital city for both Philip II and Alexander the Great. The most interesting displays in the small **Archaeological Museum** (open Tues–Sun 8.30am–3pm; admission fee) are several impressive mosaics from private houses.

# Thessaloníki

With a population of approximately one million, **Thessaloníki** is Greece's second largest city. Founded in 316BC, it has prospered ever since, helped by its pivotal location on the **Thermaic Gulf**. In 146BC it was captured by the Romans and in AD49 St Paul made converts among the city's Jewish colony. During the Byzantine period it became a major city on the Via Egnatía, the route across northern Greece connecting Constantinople with the Adriatic. The Ottomans captured the city in 1430, staying until the First Balkan War in 1912. Until the 1922 exchange of populations between Greece and Turkey, the primary characteristic of the city was its ethnic diversity, including a large Jewish community.

The major monuments remaining from Roman rule are the **Triumphal Arch of Galerius** and the **Rotunda**, which were both built by Galerius (AD250–311), the ruler of the

**Café on Thessaloníki's waterfront**

eastern half of the Roman Empire divided by Emperor Diocletian. He erected the Triumphal Arch in AD279 to celebrate his victory over the Persians. The Rotunda was completed a few years later, probably intended as his grandiose tomb, but he was buried in Bulgaria where he died in AD311. It was converted into the church of **St George** (open: Tues–Sun 8.30am–5pm) in AD379 and some 4th-century mosaics remain. The minaret is a relic of the building's use by the Ottomans as a mosque.

Dimitrios, the patron saint of Thessaloniki (feast day 26 Oct) was martyred by Galerius in AD303. The church of **St Dimítrios** (open Tues–Sat 8am–8pm, Sun 11am–8pm, Mon 1.30pm–8pm) is the largest church in Greece. The original building was constructed in the early 5th century and rebuilt in the 7th century to the same plan after being burned down. From 1491 until 1907 it was used as a mosque. Some marvellous 6th- and 7th-century mosaics survive despite the building having been badly damaged by fire in 1917.

**Large sections of Thessaloníki's city walls are still standing, including the city's symbol, the White Tower. Built in the 15th century, it was later used as an Ottoman prison and place of execution.**

Other Byzantine churches worth seeing are the **Panaghía Ahiropíetos** (5th century), the **Church of the Holy Apostles** (14th century), **Panaghía Halkéon** (1028), **St Catherine** (13th century), **Ághios Nikólaos Orfanós** (14th century) and **Aghía Sophía** (8th century). The monastery of **Vlatádhon** is believed to have been built where St Paul preached to the Thessalonians. The 5th-century church of **Ósios Davíd** nearby has a wonderful mosaic of Christ in the dome. The 1484 **Alatza Imaret Mosque** (open Tues–Fri 9am–1pm and 5pm–9pm, Sat 5pm–9pm, Sun 9am–1pm) has unusual mosaic decoration.

The excellent **Archaeological Museum** (open daily 8am–7pm, Mon noon–7pm; admission fee) has a good selection of Macedonian Hellenistic and Roman finds from throughout the region. The Gold of Macedon exhibition is particularly impressive. The museum is a short way inland from the White Tower.

The beautifully designed **Museum of Byzantine Culture** (open daily 8am– 7pm, Mon 12.30–7pm in summer; 8.30am–3pm, Mon 10.30am–5pm in winter; admission fee), across the street from the Archaeological Museum, has exemplary displays of objects from the early

Looking down to the sea from the Arch of Galerius

Byzantine period (4th to 7th centuries) until Constantinople was captured by the Fourth Crusade in 1204. Another insight into Thessaloníki's history is to be found in the **Museum of the Jewish Presence** (open Mon–Fri 9.30am–1pm).

You will find good eating throughout the city: in the newly chic **Ladhádhika** area near **Aristotélous Square**; the **Eptapyrgíou** in the upper town; and in the market area, also known as **Modiáno**. The **State Theatre of Northern Greece**, the **Vassilikó (Royal) Theatre**, the **Théatro Kípou (Garden)**, and **Théatro Dhéssos (Forest)** all provide summer programmes of concerts, dance and plays by good, sometimes very good Greek and foreign performers.

### Kirkíni

To the north and slightly east of Thessaloníki near Sidhirókastro is **Lake Kirkíni**, now an artificial lake made by damming the River Strymónas. It is one of the wetland sites protected by the Ramsar Convention and is magical, for here, particularly in spring, you can see herons and pelicans and a wide variety of waterfowl just a few metres distant.

### Halkidhikí

Halkidhikí is the wide peninsula directly southeast of Thessaloníki, with its three finger peninsulas of Kassándra, Sithonía and Mt Áthos. The **Petrálona Cave**, in which human remains from the paleolithic period were found, is now open to visitors. The beautiful beaches of **Kassándra**, such as at **Kallithéa** halfway down the eastern coast, make it the most popular resort area for Thessaloníki. The central peninsula,

**A monastery perched on the side of Mt Áthos**

**Sithonía**, is more ruggedly beautiful, with small beaches and bays. The almost encircled bay of **Koufó**, on the southern tip of Sithonía, is a wonderful place for lunch or dinner. The third peninsula is **Mt Áthos**, the Holy Mountain, reserved for monks and hermits since the 9th century and banned to women since the 11th century. The earliest monastery, the **Meghístis Lávras** (Great Lavra) was founded in 963, but most of the others were founded in the 10th and 11th centuries. If you want to visit Mt Áthos you need permission from the Greek Ministry of Foreign Affairs in Athens. For women, a view of Mt Áthos can be had from one of the tour boats that cruise around the peninsula.

## Northeast of Halkidhikí

Little remains of the ancient city of Amphipolis but, on the old road, you can still see the magnificent **Lion of Amphípolis** guarding the Strymónas River. The lion may have been built to honour one of Alexander the Great's naval commanders;

> Áthos, an independent monastic republic, bans access to women and restricts the numbers of male visitors. However, these rules fall foul of EU gender equality and freedom of passage laws, and pressure is building on Áthos to start obeying them.

what you see today was reconstructed in 1936.

**Kavála** is a busy, pretty seaport, from which ferries leave for Thásos and Samothráki as well as the other northeastern Aegean Islands. Philip II of Macedon used Kavála as the port for his city of Philippi and St Paul visited here in AD49. The Ottoman Turks occupied the city from 1391 until 1912. The **Byzantine castle** on the headland has a wonderful view of the harbour and the Ottoman aqueduct, built by Suleiman the Magnificent (1494–1566). The **Imaret**, originally a multi-domed almshouse, is now a pleasant bar-restaurant. The well-preserved **Mehmet Ali birthplace**, where he was born in

1769, is on the other side of the peninsula, providing a glimpse of 18th-century Ottoman life. Mehmet Ali was the 19th-century ruler of Egypt whose power rivalled that of the sultan and whose army, commanded by his son, Ibrahim, caused so much grief to Greece during the War of Independence.

**Philippi**, built by Philip II of Macedon, is about 15km (9 miles) northwest of Kavála. Here Mark Antony defeated Brutus and Cassius in two battles in AD42. St Paul made his first European convert, Lydia, in Philippi in AD49. Beneath **Basilica A** is a Roman crypt traditionally believed to be where St Paul was imprisoned one night until an earthquake helped convert the jailor.

> **The WWF runs an information centre in Dhadhiá and maintains an observation post from which you can see some of the birds, including 3-m (10-ft) wingspan Black Vultures, feed.**

The inland towns of Xánthi and Komotiní are centres for Greece's Pomak population, blond Muslims who may be descendants of the original Thracians. The Turkish district in **Komotiní**, with its spice and sweet shops, is a delight. Ecotourism operating out of **Xánthi** and the village of **Stavroúpoli** helps visitors see the beauties of the upper **Néstos River** and the **Haídou Forest** in the **Rodópi Mountains**.

## Alexandroúpoli

Although rather uninspiring in itself, the seaside city of Alexandroúpoli is a good base for visits to two of Greece's most interesting bird sanctuaries: the Évros Delta and Dhadhiá. The **Évros Delta** is one of Greece's 10 Ramsar protected wetland sites and, although not well organised, is home to more than 230 different species of birds. The **Dhadhiá Forest Refuge** up near **Souflí** is for raptors, large birds of prey that need space between trees and space between branches, a so-called open forest.

## South of Thessaloníki

The ancient city of **Dión** (open daily 8am–7pm; admission fee) is south of Thessaloniki below Kateríni and almost in the foothills of Mt Ólympos. The area was sacred to Olympian Zeus, but the city had sanctuaries to Demeter and Isis-Tyche. There are also fortifications, a Roman and Hellenistic theatre, and a baths complex. The city was active from the 6th century BC to the 4th century AD. The small **Archaeological Museum** (open daily 8am–7pm, Mon 12.30–7pm; admission fee) has finds from the area; the most interesting is an ancient musical instrument called the **hydraulis**.

The imposing bulk of **Mt Ólympos** (2,918m/9,568ft) dominates the horizon south of Thessaloniki; the ancient Greeks believed the mountain was home for the gods. The climb, only for experienced trekkers and climbers, is best tackled from the village of **Litóhoro**.

**Mt Ólympos seen from Litóhoro**

# THE PELOPONNESE

## Corinth and the Argolid

When driving to the Peloponnese from Athens you can easily drive over the **Corinth Canal** (opened 1893) without noticing it unless you get off the National Road at signs marked for Loutráki and cross the canal over the old bridge. The old bridge has a walkway from which you can look directly down upon the deep, sharp cut into the rock and, if you are lucky, the decks of some ship barely fitting through the narrow passage.

**Ancient Corinth** (open daily 8am–7pm; admission fee) is on the northwest bulge connecting the Peloponnese to mainland Greece. The 6th-century Doric **Temple of Apollo**, with seven of its columns still standing, is one of the oldest in Greece and is the site's centrepiece. There are also extensive

The Boúrdzi seen from Náfplio's waterfront

remains of the Roman city, including the traditional **bema** (platform) where St Paul, who was in the city in 50–51 and again in 57–58, was brought before the proconsul in 51.

The citadel of **Mycenae** (open daily 8am–7pm; admission fee), more than 3,000 years old and protected by walls of huge **polygonal stones** weighing some six tonnes each, has its own majestic grandeur, as does the famous **Lion Gate**, beneath which passed Agamemnon, his queen, Clytemnestra, their son, Orestes, and many other heroes of the Trojan War and ancient Greek tragedy. Outside the citadel are the huge beehive tombs reputed to be those of Agamemnon and Clytemnestra. The stunning gold masks and jewellery found here are on display in the National Archaeological Museum in Athens.

> The first prime minister of independent Greece was Ioannis Kapodistrias. He met a sticky end in a Náfplio street when he was assassinated by two leaders from the Máni who objected to what they saw as a concentration of power in his own hands.

Shortly before Náfplio is **Tiryns** (open Tues–Sun 8.30am–3pm; admission fee), inhabited since 5000BC but with most visible remains dating from 2500–2000BC. The walls here are some 8m (25ft) thick, and the largest stones weigh 14 tonnes.

**Náfplio** was Greece's first formal capital, and its Venetian and 19th-century architecture makes it one of the country's prettiest towns. The city lies along the shore beneath the huge Venetian fortress of **Palamídi** (open daily 8am–6.45pm; admission fee) that dominates the heights behind. The **Boúrdzi fortress** in the harbour was built by the Venetians in two stages, in the 16th and 18th centuries. Just inside the front door to the church of **Ághios Spyrídonas** (1702) is a small glass frame covering the hole made by the bullet that killed the first president of Greece, Ioánnis Kapodístrias, in 1831.

▶ **Ancient Epídavros** (open daily 8.30am–7pm; admission fee) with a small **museum** (open daily 8am–7pm; Mon noon–7pm) is primarily famous for the wonderful acoustics of its ancient theatre, in which plays are performed each year as part of the Athens Festival, but in antiquity it was known for its **Sanctuary of Asclepios**, now being carefully restored by the Greek Department of Antiquities. The site is diverse and interesting, and has its mystery in the circular **Tholos**.

**Paleá Epídavros** is a small village port with a couple of pleasant *tavérnes* by the water.

From **Lighourió** you can drive down to the east coast of the Argolid at Fanári and then continue along the shore to **Méthana** or **Galatás**, across from the island of **Póros**. **Pórto Héli**, in the southern corner, is a middling resort town from which you can easily cross over to the island of **Spétses**.

> The ancient Spartans had a very different society from their Athenian counterparts and sometime enemies. Reliant on a large body of serfs, known as the helots, to support a military elite, the Spartans prioritised military prowess and the rule of the strong above the arts or any sort of democratic system.

## South of Argos

The market town of **Árgos** has ancient remains not easily seen and is crowned with a Byzantine-Crusader-Venetian-Ottoman castle more impressive at a distance than up close. Nearby **Lérna** (Lerni; open Tues–Sun 8.30am–3pm; admission fee) is one of the oldest settlements in Greece, where Hercules killed the Hydra.

**Leonídhi** stands at the mouth of a huge red gash cut in the flanks of Mt Parnona by a mountain torrent. It is an unspoilt place with its harbour-hamlet of **Pláka** down on the beach at the edge of a rich alluvial plain with orange groves and vegetable plots.

Behind Leonídi the road climbs into the mountains to the medieval town of **Yeráki**, built by the crusading French in the 13th century.

The walled medieval town of **Monemvásia**, right on the water at the foot of a huge rock, was an important Byzantine port. William de Villehardouin occupied it for 13 years in the mid-13th century. In the 15th century it was controlled by the Pope, then by the Venetians (1464–1540 and 1690–1715) and the Ottoman Turks (1540–1690 and 1715–1821). Once you have passed through the uninter-esting new town, cross the

The rooftops of Monemvásia

causeway and enter the gate to wander through the wonder-ful narrow streets among the many beautifully restored houses of the old town. The **upper town** has long been aban-doned, but the view – if you can make the climb – is unequalled, and the late 13th- to early 14th-century church of **Aghía Sofía** has been well restored.

## Sparta

**Ancient Sparta** left few remains, as is fitting for a city that relied on the strength of its fighting men and disdained defensive walls, but there is a small **archaeological museum** (open Tues–Sun 8.30am–3pm; admission fee). Nearby **Mystrás** (open daily 8am–7pm; admission fee), unlike declining Constantinople, was a flourishing Byzantine centre in the 15th century and provided the last, heroic Byzantine emperor, Constantine, to lead the final, doomed defence of Constantinople against the Ottoman Turks in 1453. Several churches remain, with their domes and patterned brickwork, in particular the church of **Ághios Dimítrios**, in which a double-headed eagle marks the spot where the last Byzantine emperor was crowned.

## The Máni

**Tower houses at Vathiá in the Máni**

The central of the three peninsulas that make up the southern Peloponnese is a largely bare rock whose inhabitants are fiercely independent. The region's blood feuds have left a fascinating legacy of defensive architecture and women's laments. You enter through **Gýthio** (Yíthio), a small harbour town with the small island where Paris and Helen spent their first night together. After the larger town of **Areópolis** on the west coast, the road goes through poor villages near the square stone towers the Maniots built to protect themselves from belligerent neighbouring families. Prehistoric remains were found in the **Dhiroú Caves**, but there's usually a long queue for the boat tour. **Vathiá** is a dramatic, largely deserted tower village towards the southern tip of the Máni.

## Southwest Peloponnese

At **Koróni** on the east and **Methóni** on the west side of the westernmost peninsula there are two wonderful Venetian castles, both built in the 13th century to protect Venetian trade with the Byzantine and, later, the Ottoman empires.

The well-protected **Bay of Navarino** is where Greece became independent. In 1827 the combined British, French and Russian fleet entered the bay in which the Ottoman navy was sheltering. The battle, apparently started by accident, ended after 53 Ottoman ships had been sunk and 6,000 Ottoman seamen had been killed. The allied fleet did not lose a single ship, although 174 men were killed. Ottoman rule in Greece was over. The uninhabited island of **Sfaktíria** is famous in ancient Greek history as being the place where the Spartan survivors of a long siege by Athenian forces in 420BC surrendered, an unheard of development, instead of fighting to the death.

A 13th-century **Venetian castle**, some of it built on ancient foundations, is at the top of the promontory facing Sfaktíria. Just to the north is a wonderful, protected circular bay, called Voidokiliá (ox-belly) where it is thought Telemachus, the son of Odysseus, beached his boat while on his way to ask for news of his father. Above the beach is a very early beehive tomb and, on the other side, a cave in which Nestor kept his cattle, the same cave in which Hermes is supposed to have hidden the cattle he stole from Apollo.

**A stormy day over the Máni**

The excavated remains of **Nestor's Palace**, nothing much more than a metre high, are on a wooded spur looking south over the Bay of Navarino. You can clearly see the hearth in the main room where Telemachus would have been received, and you can see the clay jars where olive oil was stored – even the painted bath; mythology made tangible.

Most of the coast from Kyparissía to Káto Ahaía near Patras is one long beach, only occasionally interrupted. The extensive sanctuary, not a city, of **Ancient Olympia** (open daily 8am–7pm; admission fee), where the Olympic Games were held every four years from 776BC until AD393, is inland from Pýrgos. For all the frenetic activity in both the ancient and the modern Olympic Games, the site today is a quiet, shaded place with, notably, **temples of Zeus and Hera** and, of course the **ancient stadium**. The most famous statue in the **museum** (open Tues–Sun 8am–7pm, Mon noon–7pm; admission fee) is the classical **statue of Hermes** holding the infant Dionsyos by Praxiteles. Among the ancient armour on display is the helmet that belonged to Miltiades, the victorious Athenian commander at the battle of Marathon.

The castle of **Hlemoútzi**, near Kyllíni, was the headquarters of the Villehardouins, the most prominent of the Frankish families who ruled the Peloponnese, then known as the Morea, after the fall of Constantinople to the Fourth Crusade in 1204. Built in 1220–23, captured by the Byzantines in 1427, and occupied and refortified by the Ottomans after 1460, it is the best preserved of the many castles built by the Franks in the Peloponnese.

## Arcadia

After Trípoli, the main city in Arcadia is **Megalópoli**, remarkable primarily for its appalling power station chimneys spewing smoke from its brown-coal burning furnaces.

Fortunately, not far to the northwest is **Karítina**, a sleepy medieval hill town with a Frankish castle. This one was built in 1254, sold to the Byzantines in 1320, and used by the Greek leader Kolokotronis as a base in his operations against Ibrahim Pasha during the Greek War of Independence.

**Inscription at Ancient Olympia**

The ancient city of **Górtys** is near the village of Atsíholos north of Karítina in the Loúsios River valley. The dirt track goes down to the fast flowing river, a small Byzantine chapel, and remains of an Asclepeion and baths, perhaps dating to the 4th century BC. The defensive walls of the acropolis occupying the heights were built during the Macedonian period. A 40-minute walk will take you up to the Prodhrómou Monastery hanging under the cliffs.

South of the pretty village of Andrítsana, high above the River Alfíos, is the Doric **Temple of Apollo Epikourios** at **Bassae** (Vassae; open daily 6am–9pm; admission fee), built in 450–447BC, before the Parthenon in Athens. The temple is famous because it is well preserved and in such a dramatic, remote location. Since the mid-1980s, however, the entire edifice has been covered by a startling tent to protect water damage to the foundations. The cella frieze is in the British Museum

# ARGO-SARONIC GULF ISLANDS

## Égina (Aegina)

Égina is the most accessible holiday island from Athens, with regular boats here taking just 1½hrs (hydrofoils take only 40 minutes). The capital of the country for slightly over a year (1827), Égina is now a major producer of pistachios, which you will find sold virtually all along the waterfront.

**Kolóna** near Égina town has a 6th-century BC Doric column still standing, and just outside the small museum is a reconstructed mosaic floor from an early synagogue. The other and much more impressive archaeological site is the Doric **Temple of Aphaia** above **Aghía Marína** on the island's western coast, dating from 490BC. The site, surrounded by trees and overlooking the sea, is beautiful and the temple is one of the best example of Archaic Greek architecture.

**The Temple of Aphaia**

Aghía Marína below the temple has two pleasant small beaches, hotels, restaurants, fast-food eateries and souvenir shops in abundance. The small well-protected port of **Pérdhika** in the island's southern corner is well known for the good fish *tavérnes* lining the one built-up side of the port, but Pérdhika also provides easy access, by boat, to the small island of **Moní** where there is a beautiful small beach.

After Arab raiders sacked Égina town in 896, the islanders moved inland and built what is now known as **Paleohóra**, the old village. In 1537 the town was badly damaged by Kheir el-Din Barbarossa, and in 1654 it was briefly occupied by the Venetians. The townspeople began moving back down to Égina town early in the 19th century and gradually Paleochóra was abandoned. It now consists only of 38 churches, many of them still containing wall paintings.

Égina is not well endowed with sandy beaches, although there is one at **Marathón**, about a third of the way up from Pérdhika up towards Égina town. There are narrow sand beaches on the northern coast, at **Vathíos** and **Souvála**, and smaller stretches of beach along the eastern coast. Many people swim off the rocks at the **lighthouse** past Kolóna.

## Póros

The experience of travelling by ship, not hydrofoil, through the channel separating Póros from the Peloponnese will be hard to forget, for the ship comes so close to Poros town that the upper decks put you on eye level with the upper storeys of the island houses. The island has one archaeological site, the ancient city of **Kalauria** and the **Sanctuary of Poseidon**, now being excavated by Swedish archaeologists. There are a couple of beaches towards the **Zoödóhos Pighí Monastery** along the southern side of the main bulk of the island, but the better beaches are in the other direction, towards **Megálo Neório** and beyond.

## Ídhra (Hydra)

Ídhra's beautiful harbour

Ídhra is famous in modern Greek history because of the naval fighting power its wealthy shipping captains put up against the Ottomans during the Greek War of Independence. Today it is known for its beautiful **harbour** and town, carefully kept free of cars. All the large grey stone mansions around the harbour were built early in the 19th century. The **Panaghía Monastery** and its clock tower were built in the 1770s, incorporating considerable building material from the Sanctuary of Poseidon on Póros. The island has some wonderful restaurants and small hotels.

## Spétses

Gentle, wooded Spétses also had considerable wealth from shipping in the 18th and 19th centuries and contributed naval power, largely the ships commanded by its female admiral **Bouboulina**, to the independence struggle. The **Dápia**, Spétses' small harbour, is the island's bustling heart, with fine small streets and shops for wandering. The **Old Harbour**, 1.5km (1 mile) to the southeast still has an operating shipyard building large wooden boats. The town stretches along the northwest coast to the Anargýrios Koryialénos School. John Fowles taught here and set his *The Magus* on the island, but the school no longer operates. The best beaches are at **Aghía Marína**, **Ághii Anárghyri** and **Aghía Paraskeví**, and at **Zogeriá**.

# THE IONIAN ISLANDS

## Corfu

**Corfu** (Kérkyra) remains remarkably beautiful. The island is well watered, therefore green, all year long, and in spring wild flowers carpet the ground. Corfu has been inhabited since palaeolithic times, but it enters the historical record when Corinth founded a colony on the island in 734BC. The only pivotal role it played in classical history was to spark the Second Peloponnesian War (431–404BC) when Athens helped the islands revolt against Corinthian rule. Under Roman rule from 229BC, Corfu supported Antony against Octavian at the battle of Actium in 31BC and had her monuments razed as punishment.

**Coffee in the Listón arcade, Corfu Town**

Venetian rule (1386–1797) left an indelible mark on Corfu. In 1623 the Venetians began to encourage olive tree cultivation, and the sheer abundance of olive groves remains one of the most striking aspects of the landscape. Some of the buildings are Venetian in style, as is the layout of Corfu Town.

The island was then ruled by France for two years, after which it became part of the Septinsular Republic, virtually a Russian-Ottoman protectorate (1799–1807). France ruled again in 1807–14, then came the British (1814–64). Thereafter Corfu became part of Greece. It was never under Ottoman control.

The meandering streets of **Corfu Town** wander between 17th- and 18th-century Italianate townhouses, most of them with ground-floor shops selling an endless variety of goods. The large open **esplanade** *(spianáda)*, originally kept open to provide a line of fire between the medieval town and the **Old Fort**, is now the city's extensive park, used by the islanders for open-air concerts and playing cricket. The **Liston**, the two handsome apartment blocks facing the esplanade, were inspired by the rue de Rivoli in Paris. A statue of Ioannis Kapodistrias, the first president of independent Greece who was born on Corfu in 1776, stands in the southwest corner of the esplanade.

> The two English authors most closely associated with Corfu are the (very different) brothers Gerald and Lawrence Durrell. The former is known for his amusing accounts of his childhood enthusiasm for the island's natural history, the latter for his travel writing and novels.

Behind the Liston on Guilford Street is the **Town Hall**, originally built in 1663 for visiting merchants. A **monument** honouring Francesco Morosini, the Venetian commander whose bombardment of the Acropolis in Athens in 1687 ignited the stored munitions and blew away most of the Parthenon, is on the building's east wall. The church of **Ághios Spyrídon** (1596) houses the remains of Corfu's patron saint, after whom most of the island's men are named. South of the esplanade the **Archaeological Museum** (open Mon noon–7pm, Tues–Sun 8am–7pm; admission fee), houses the archaic **Gorgon and panther pediment**, the most extraordinarily endearing statuary of archaic Greek art.

**Kontókali**, on the north coast near Corfu Town, is packed with tourist restaurants and bars. **Kalámi**, 32km (20 miles) along the coast, is where Lawrence Durrell lived before World

War II. At **Ághios Stéfanos**, 6km (4 miles) further on, there is a pretty little harbour with several lovely restaurants. Much of the north coast is open beach. **Kassiópi** is the prettiest, **Rhódha** the most developed. The drive back through the mountains is beautiful, with the landscape punctuated by olive groves and cypress trees.

The famous double bays of **Paleokastrítsa** on the island's west coast are packed in the summer, better viewed from above at the **Bella Vista** café outside the village of **Lákones** in the mountains. **Glyfáda Beach** and **Ághios Ghórdis** are resorts along the west coast.

The small chapel of Ághios Arsénios near Kalámi

Activities and development are more organised at Glyfada than at Ághios Ghórdis. There's less crowded swimming off the beautiful rocks at Drástis Point below Sidhári in the northwest or the long stretch of undeveloped beach at **Ághios Yeórgos** below Lake Korissíon on the southwest coast.

## Paxí and Andípaxi

The small island of **Paxí** has several beautiful villages, three wonderful small ports, and many lovely beaches, notably **Kipiádi** and **Ahái**. The far smaller island of **Andípaxi** has only a handful of inhabitants, two *tavérnes*, and the wonderful beaches of Vatoúmi and Vríka.

## Lefkádha

Lefkádha is large, green and mountainous, deeply incised on the south and east by bays and blessed by a line of beautiful beaches along most of its northern and western coasts. Along with all the Ionian Islands, it was ruled by a succession of foreign powers from the Middle Ages onwards: Franks (1300–1479), Ottomans (1479–1684), Venetians (1684–1797), French (1797–1798), Russians and Ottomans (1798–1800), Septinsular Republic (1800–1807), French (1807–1810) and British (1810–1864). The old canal separating the island from the mainland was on the east side of the 14th-century **Fort Santa Maura**. The present canal, cut in 1905, put the fort on the mainland. The floating drawbridge makes it possible for you to get on and off the island whatever the weather.

**Lefkádha town** has something of a medieval appearance, although the main street is full of new shopfronts. The upper

**Sappho's Leap at the impressive cliffs of Cape Lefkátas**

floors of many houses are covered in sheet metal, often painted in pastel colours, to keep out the rain and humidity. There are 34 extraordinary churches on the island, 19 of them in town, all built a few years after 1684 when the Venetians expelled the Ottomans. They look like scaled-down baroque churches, not at all like traditional Greek Orthodox churches, and their icons and wall paintings are Renaissance in style. The oldest, **Ághios Spyrídhon** on the main square, was built in 1685.

The eastern side of the island, protected from the prevailing winds, is gentle and wooded, with stretches of shore you can reach for swimming. **Lygiá** is a small, pretty fishing harbour and **Nikiána** has shops and accommodation. The bustling tourist town of **Nydhrí** is the biggest draw on this coast – the harbour is well protected and it is right next to the beautiful, almost completely enclosed **Bay of Vlyhós**.

On the southern coast, past Vlyhós, is the little village of **Póros**, with a stretch of usually uncrowded pebble beach. The next bay, **Syvotá**, is curved and dramatically narrow, with a small fishing village. The fishing village of **Vassilikí**, with restaurants and cafés along the quay, is a pleasant place to stop. The long open stretch of beach just past the village is protected from high seas by the long peninsula leading down to Sappho's Leap. It is a good beach for swimming and windsurfing. The little sand beach of **Pírto Katsíki** is in the middle of the peninsula, on the west coast. The beach is beautiful, reached only by a winding road down the mountainside, but the road has brought visitors. Go down only if you see from above that the area is not packed with cars. The dramatic and dangerous cliffs of **Sappho's Leap**, now capped by a modern lighthouse, is at the southern end of the peninsula.

Much of the northern and northwestern coasts consist of beautiful, long stretches of beach. **Káthisma**, now fitted out with beach umbrellas at one end but still unencumbered at its southern end, is southwest of the once isolated, now inundated tiny village of **Ághios Nikítas**. It has some lovely hotels, but the village can hardly be approached in peak summer season. The very long stretch of beautiful beach from Ághios Nikítas to the northeast can be reached only on foot and is used by few people.

The stretch of beach after the shallow salt-water lagoon known as the Yíro, and shortly before the mountain comes down sharply to the sea, is known as **Ághios Ioánnis**, after a tiny 13th-century chapel near the shore. Most people go to the small organised beach at Ághios Ioánnis, where there are only a few metres between the road and the water, but if you walk up over the dunes anywhere along the lagoon or by the old windmills you will come down to the sea.

> **The southern Ionian Islands are some of the last Mediterranean breeding grounds of the loggerhead turtle. Their nesting sites are seriously under threat from tourism development. The Greek society, Archelon, runs a protection programme (*visit* <www.archelon.gr>).**

The largest inland village, in the mountains, is **Karyá**, known for embroidery.

## Kefaloniá

Kefaloniá is the largest of the Ionian Islands and has their tallest mountain (Mt Énos), its own fir (*Abies cephalonica*), and beautiful beaches. **Argostóli**, the island's capital, is a good base from which to explore. Most of the buildings on the island were built after a devastating earthquake in 1953, so a visit to the **Korgialenio Historical and Cultural Museum** (open Mon–Sat 9am–2pm; admission fee) will give you a glimpse of Kefaloniá's past. The area southwest of Argostóli known as Livathó is green and flowered and dotted with prosperous villages such as **Metaxáta** (Byron

**A baby loggerhead turtle** *(Caretta caretta)*

stayed here), **Kalligáta** (Calliga wines) and **Peratáta** (17th-century wall paintings in the monastery of St Andrews). The impressive Venetian walls of the **Castle of St George** look out over the villages of **Travliáta** and Peratáta. **Skála**, in the southwest of the island, is a growing resort with a beautiful long stretch of golden sand. Boats from Kyllíni on the Peloponnese dock at **Póros**, further north. Sámi, primarily a place where ferries land, is near the impressive **Drogharáti Cave** and the beautiful lake cave of **Mellissáni**, from which water flows beneath the island to emerge near Argostóli.

The northern part of the island is more abruptly mountainous, often barren, and untouched by the 1953 earthquake. **Ássos** is a beautiful, tiny port beneath a huge Venetian fortress on the round peninsula beyond the narrow connecting strip of land. Once a fishing village, **Fiskárdo** is a carefully preserved jewel now thriving on tourism. Mýrtos Beach, south of Ássos, is strikingly beautiful.

**Kefallonián pines**

The **Pallíki peninsula**, west of Argostóli, has some good sandy beaches, notably **Mégas Lákkos** and **Xí**, and a pebble beach at **Petaní**.

## Itháki (Ithaca)

Although there is no archaeological evidence to support their belief, the islanders are convinced that their island is ancient Ithaca, the home of Odysseus. Many places on the island are named to fit the myth.

Whatever its mythological status, Ithaca is rugged and beautiful, with few beaches and not a great deal of tourist development. The port of **Vathý** lies at the end of a very deep bay on the east coast. It is quiet during the day, but at night several restaurants and bars move their tables onto the quay and the place comes to life.

The **Arethoússa Spring** is identified as the place where Odysseus hid until his son arrived to help him throw out Penelope's suitors. The mountain village of **Perahóra** is near the islands' deserted medieval capital. The road from Vathý over **Mt Etós** to **Pisaetós** passes near 8th-century BC **Alalkomenae**, once thought to be Odysseus's palace.

**Stavrós**, in the northern part of the island, is the second largest town. Below Stavrós to the west is the **Bay of Pólis**, a pleasant small beach. The **Katharón Monastery**, below the largely deserted village of **Anóghi**, has a superb view to the south towards Vathý. The view from the chapel at the end of the road past the village of **Exoghí** is wonderful, and well worth making the trip for.

# Zákynthos

Zákynthos, with wide green lowlands governing most of the eastern part of the island, is gentler than the other Ionian Islands. The thriving town, carefully rebuilt, has a distinct Venetian air about it thanks to the 17th-century church of **Ághios Dionýsios**, the island's patron saint, and its campanile. The church was one of only three buildings in town that survived the 1953 earthquake. The large open square where the ships dock is Platía Solomoú, named after the 19th-century Greek poet who wrote the words to the national anthem.

The wide bay of **Laganá** is a package tourist enclave, with hotels and dozens of restaurants and bars, all of which, it seems, stay happily open all night. The gentle sands, however, have long been used as a breeding place for loggerhead turtles, *Caretta caretta*. The whole bay is now protected as the Marine National Park of Zákynthos, and the Sea Turtle Protection Society patrols the beach to protect the nests; it also operates an information booth.

The sandy beaches in the southern part of the island are very easy to reach, and those along the Vassilikos Peninsula

---

## Captain Corelli Caused a Din

A publishing sensation in the UK, the novel *Captain Corelli's Mandolin* by Louis de Berniers has had a rather more tepid reception in Greece. Set on the the island of Kefalloniá during World War II, it follows the fortunes of a village throughout the Italian, and then German occupations. So far so good. What has raised the ire of many in Greece is in its portrayal of the Greek resistance fighters in a less than heroic light. Opponents of the book argue that it skews the history of the resistance, widely regarded as national saviours by the Greeks.

are lovely. The impressively beautiful **Blue Caves** need to be visited by *caique* from **Ághios Nikólaos**, but the west coast of the island is dotted with spectacular small beaches at the foot of limestone cliffs. The most famous of these beaches, **Navághio (Shipwreck) Beach**, can be visited only by boat, but it can be seen from the nearby monastery of Aghíou Yeorghíou Gremón (St George of the Cliffs).

## Kýthira

Kýthira is the southern sister of the Ionian Islands. Emigration has taken much of the population away, so many villages are empty, or almost empty. Most boats land at the new port of **Dhiakófti**. The

Ághios Dionýsios, Zákynthos

island's abandoned medieval capital, reminiscient of Mystrás, is near **Potamós**, the largest village. Most visitors head for **Kapsáli**, the beautiful double-bay port in the south. Just above Kapsáli you will pass through **Hóra**, with its Venetian castle. The view from here is excellent. **Mylopótamos** is a lovely inland village set in a small valley with a stream. Less than a kilometre away are the remains of **Káto Hóra**, the site of a small Venetian fortress complete with a sculpted lion and several small churches. Also nearby is the **Cave of St Sophia**.

# THE CYCLADES ISLANDS

This circular group of more than 20 islands, rocky and often barren, seems to reduce life to the fundamental elements of earth, sky, wind and water we find irresistibly compelling. This generates a stark, incomparable beauty occasionally punctuated by modest white homes and churches amid the grandeur. Below is a selection of them.

## Ándros

The northernmost of the Cyclades, **Ándros** is largely barren to the north and well-watered by springs in the south. Boats land at **Gávrio**, on the west coast, after which most visitors head for **Batsí**, once a small fishing village and now a major resort. After the road turns inland to the northeast you pass through rolling green countryside dotted with villages and extraordinary

**Traditional Cycladic architecture, Mýkonos**

medieval dovecotes. Springs gush out of the hillside at the villages of **Ménites** and **Apikía**, the latter being the source for the Sariza spring water. **Ándros town (Hóra)** is on the east coast. The small **Venetian fort** was built in the early 13th century and some of the houses in the maze of narrow streets in the lower section of town were built under Byzantine rule. The upper town has beautiful **18th- and 19th-century mansions** and two excellent museums, the **Archaeological Museum of Ándros** and the **Ándros Museum of Modern Art**, which presents shows every summer.

**A modern café on Sýros**

The village of **Steniés** to the north has abundant water, beautiful flowers and trees, an impressive 17th-century tower-mansion, and the pebble beach of Yialyiá nearby. **Korthí**, to the south, has good beaches, and on the way you will see many of the Andriote dovecotes.

## Kéa (Tziá)

**Kéa**, also known as **Tziá**, is located off the coast of Sounion and can be reached in only about 2½hrs from Athens. It has become a weekend destination for Athenians, who are building more and more houses along the western coast. **Vourkári**, within the island's large natural harbour, provides safe anchorage for many yachts and a solid line of restaurants and bars. The town, **Hóra** or **Ioulídha**, up in the mountain behind the harbour is quite pretty, and it has its share of bars and restaurants. In antiquity the island was heavily populated, there were four independent cities, and you can discern the remains of ancient terracing over much of the island. There are some serviceable beaches on the east coast, but the more beautiful beaches, **Spáthi** and **Sykamía**, are on the west coast.

## Tínos

**Tínos** is known primarily for its large church of the **Panaghía Evangelístria** (Our Lady of the Annunciation). The church's icon allegedly performs miracles, notably healing the sick. Many come here to be healed, particularly on the Virgin's day, 15 August, in person or by proxy, crawling on hands and knees from the dock to the church. Because of the island's religious nature, its development has been more subdued. Some of the inland villages, particularly on the west coast, such as **Kardhianí** and **Istérna**, are quite beautiful, and the dovecotes here are at least as impressive as the dovecotes on Ándros.

> The Cyclades were home to one of the earliest settled societies in Europe. Their most striking artefacts are the stylised marble figurines familiar from replicas found in tourist shops. Their function is unknown; theories range from them being ancestors to divinities.

## Mýkonos and Delos

For foreigners, **Mýkonos** is the most famous island in the Cyclades, extremely busy throughout the summer. The harbour town with its winding streets both to block the wind and confuse attackers, is extraordinarily beautiful, the flagstones outlined with whitewash and the shops offering the best of Greek craftsmanship along with internationally famous brands. The many good restaurants and bars and clubs here can keep you happily occupied. Otherwise, basically, Mýkonos offers beaches – wonderful stretches of

**Petros the pelican,
the mascot of Mýkonos**

gentle sand that are mostly organised, meaning you pay for the umbrella and reclining chair. **Ornós**, **Platýs Yialós**, **Psarroú** and **Ághios Stéfanos** are topless beaches. Both **Paradise** and **Super Paradise** were for nudists, Super Paradise for gays, but these distinctions have broken down. **Eliá** is also a nudist beach. If the winds are southerly, go to **Pánormos** on the northern coast, where there are no umbrellas but a good *taverna*.

Ancient **Delos** (Dílos; open Tues–Sun 8.30am– 5pm; admission fee), where Leto gave birth to Apollo and Artemis on the hill called **Mt Kynthos**, is a 30-minute boat ride from Mýkonos. It was occupied from the third millennium BC and a major religious and commercial centre from 700BC until the 3rd century AD. No one lives on the island, which has been excavated for years by the French School of Archaeology. The most photographed of the extensive remains are five 7th-century BC **stone lions**.

## Sérifos

**Sérifos**, still not much developed for tourism, has the spectacular white town of **Hóra** perched on the mountain overlooking the harbour and good beaches at Psilí Ámmos, and Gánema. Livadhákia, the nearest good beach to Hóra, can be crowded.

# Náxos

The island of **Náxos** is closely associated with Ariadne, the
daughter of King Minos of Crete who helped Theseus escape
from the labyrinth and his encounter with the minotaur. Theseus took Ariadne with him from Crete but abandoned her on
Náxos, where Dionysos, the god of wine and the theatre,
found her and married her. The small island where they met
is just to the north of the harbour capital, **Hóra**, and is now
joined to the main island by a narrow spit of land. On top of
the small island are the remains of a 6th-century BC Ionic
Temple of Apollo, with its huge portal, now the island's
symbol, still standing.

Hóra's thriving harbourfront is lined with shops, restaurants and banks, but the hill behind has the old medieval
streets with arched passageways leading up to the 13th-
century **castle** built by the Venetian Marco Sanudo. The
edifice in which the **archaeological museum** is housed
used to be the **French School**, founded in 1627 to provide
schooling free of charge to both Catholic and Greek Orthodox students; these included, late in the 19th century, the
writer Nikos Kazantzakis.

Náxos is the largest of the
Cyclades, and as soon as
you leave Hóra you will find
it a surprisingly green,
agricultural island, belying
the standardised Cycladic
image of barren hills and
white buildings. The white
buildings are here, to be
sure, but they seem some-
what incongruous, and
gentler, against the green.
The best beaches are down

**The Temple of Apollo**

the coast to the south, first **Pláka**, now increasingly built up, and then down to **Mikró Vígla** and beyond. The inland village of **Filotí** provides a wonderful view over the extensive green groves of the **Tragéa**, containing 12 small villages and many Byzantine churches. In summer the lovely village of **Apíranthos**, higher on Mt Zeus, is a wonderful place for a cool evening meal. The partly restored 6th-century **Temple of Demeter**, comfortably set in a wide green valley south of **Áno Sangrí**, is one of the most beautiful temples in the country.

The other ancient sites not to be missed are the 10.5-m (34-ft) **Apollo** *kouros* (statue), probably dating to *circa* 600BC,

**A village clinging to the side of a Náxos Mountain**

left lying in the quarry probably because a crack developed. The *kouros* lies in the hill above the village of Apóllonas on the island's otherwise unremarkable northern coast. The younger and smaller **Flerio** *kouros*, this one abandoned with a broken leg, is much nearer Hóra, by the small village of Mýli.

## Páros

**Páros**, famous in antiquity for its brilliant, slightly translucent white marble, is a working agricultural island as well as a tourist resort. It has three main towns: the port and capital **Parikía** on the west coast; the fishing village of **Náoussa** in the north; and the farming mountain town of **Léfkes** in the centre; and a few small villages. Parikía is where the nightlife is concentrated, but the town also has the Church of the Hundred Doors, Ekatontapyliani, one of the oldest churches in the world, first built in the early 4th century by Emperor Constantine and reconstructed in the 6th century by Emperor Justinian.

**Náoussa**, once a sleepy little fishing village on the northern coast, is now swamped with boutiques, bars and restaurants, as many as possible squeezed onto the little harbourfront. But it is still very pretty, and a good place to have an evening drink or a meal. **Kolymbíthres**, with its wind-eroded rocks, is the best-known beach nearby. Some nudists use the partly commercialised beach of **Monastéri**. **Léngeri** and **Sánta María** are less crowded.

**Léfkes**, a safe distance from the sea up in the mountains, was the island's capital but is now a beautiful, quiet mountain village.

> The white cube architecture of the Cyclades not only appears to perfectly complement the environment of dry, rugged land and deep blue sea, but has also been influential to modernist architects. These include Le Corbusier, who was particularly entranced by Hóra on Folégandros.

## Sífnos

**Sífnos** is small, green and dainty, her 2,400 population able only with difficulty to handle the summer rush. On the trip from the port of Kamáres to the capital of **Apollonía** you will see two-storey dovecotes, small chapels set in the hillside, a Hellenistic watchtower, ruined windmills, and narrow terraces holding golden grains, olive trees or grapevines. Apollonía, which needs to be explored on foot, is an amalgam of six villages now grown into one. A marble column in the courtyard of the 18th-century church of the **Panaghía**

**Ouranofóra** is from the 7th-century BC Temple of Apollo, after whom the village is named. To the north, **Artemónas**, with neoclassical houses, is the island's most beautiful village. The depleted ancient silver mines at **Ághios Sóstis** made the island wealthy during the Archaic period. **Plaýs Yialós**, **Fárou** and **Vathý** are the most popular beaches.

## Mílos
**Mílos**, famous for its spectacular geology, has, among other attractions, a huge bay, some pretty villages (**Klíma**), good windsurfing (**Pollónia**), lovely beaches (**Chivadoliméni**, **Rivári**) and the rock-columns in the sea at **Kléftiko**.

The wonderful Cycladic
architecture of Ía, Santoríni

## Íos

Íos has long been a paradise for the
young crowd, but the police have
been cracking down recently. Most
of the considerable action is at
**Yialós**, **Hóra** or **Mylopótamos
(Mylopóta)**. The best beaches are
**Mylopóta**, **Manganári**, **Loúkes**,
**Aghía Theodóti**, and **Psathí**.
Homer's reputed **tomb** is in the
north of the island, far enough
away for him to get some rest.

## Santoríni

**Santoríni (Thíra)** is a volcanic ◄
island that gives you one of the
most impressive sights in the world
when you enter the caldera harbour by ship. The high, sharp cliffs
of the western coast enclose the very deep water of the harbour like a jagged crescent moon, and many believe this to
be the site of ancient Atlantis, destroyed by a gigantic volcanic eruption in approximately 1500BC. At **Akrotíri** (open
daily 7.30am–7pm in summer, Tues–Sun 8.30am–3pm in
winte; admission fee), on the southern point of the crescent,
remains of an impressive Minoan settlement, including two-
storey buildings, indoor plumbing and gracious wall paintings,
have been excavated. The main town of **Fíra** (or **Thíra** or
**Hóra**), built on the cliff edge, is where most of the island's
nightlife is located and is crowded from June to August.
Both Fíra and the smaller, more up-market village of **Ía** on

the northern point of the crescent are spectacularly beautiful, with their white houses clinging to the cliff edge providing incomparable views. **Megalohóri**, near Fíra, has not been swamped by tourism, and **Emborió** has a largely intact medieval fortress. The beaches are on the western and southern coasts. The black sand beach of Kamári is impressive, but often crowded, and the sand can get very hot.

## Amorgós

The small island of **Amorgós** is dramatically mountainous, with some lovely white villages, several good beaches (**Eyiáli**, **Levrosós**, **Psilí Ámmos**, **Hohlakás**, **Martézi**, **Plákes**, **Moúros**, as well as on the islet of **Gramvoúsa**). It also has the most beautiful monastery in the Cyclades, the white, 10th-century **Panaghía Hozoviótissas**, set into the cliff 300m (984ft) above the sea.

## Folégandros

Although mountainous Folégandros has only two villages (**Hóra** and **Áno Meriá**) and 700 inhabitants, it has burst into tourism in recent years, filling its spectacular clifftop village of **Hóra** with *tavérnes* and bars. The prettiest beach is Kátergo in the southeast. Below Angáli on the western coast of the island's waist are Ághios Nikólaos, Ambéli and Livadháki.

## Anáfi

Anáfi is a quiet island, with most of its 300 inhabitants living in **Hóra** and the remainder living in the little port of **Ághios Nikólaos** and **Klisídi**. It has no nightclubs or hotels but does have wonderful beaches, notably **Roúkouna**, along the southern shore. From the monastery of **Kalamiótissa** on top of the 450-m (1,476-ft) high pyramid of rock at the island's eastern tip you can see as far as Kálymnos in the Dodecanese Islands to the east and Crete to the south.

# SPORADES ISLANDS

## Skiáthos

Heavily developed but still quite beautiful, **Skiathos**, right off the heel of Mt Pélion, has one town; a famous 19th-century author, Papadiamantis; two preserved monasteries, including the beautiful 18th-century **Evanglistréas Monastery**; and 62 beaches, some of the best in Greece. To list only four: **Koukounarís** is a highly developed, popular resort; the **Big** and **Little Banana** beaches are for nudists; and **Lalária**, which can be reached only by boat, is a beautiful pebble beach.

**The beach of Kastáni on Skópelos**

## Skópelos

Skópelos is less heavily developed than Skiáthos, and its two towns, **Skiáthos** and **Glóssa**, both looking down over the water and both mostly of traditional white architecture and tile roofs, are prettier. Of the main beaches of **Stáfylos**, **Agnóntas**, **Limnonári**, **Pánormos** and **Miliá**, Pánormos is the most commercialised.

## Alónissos

After the island's main town, **Hóra**, was damaged by an earthquake in 1965, the residents moved down to where the boats land, **Patitíri**, a concrete collection of buildings putting on its best face with potted plants and flowering vines. Many foreigners, mostly German and English, have purchased and carefully restored abandoned houses in Hóra. The Monk Seal Protection Society is based in **Stení Vála**, and the northern Sporades are a marine wildlife reserve to protect the small remaining population of Mediterranean monk seals. It is fitting that the island is relatively quiet. The best beaches near Patitíri are **Rousoúm Yialós**, **Kokkinnókastro**, **Leftós Yialós**, **Miliá**, **Hryssí Miliá**, and **Vótsi**. To the northeast are **Glýfa**, **Kalamákia** and **Ághios Dimítrios**; to the south are **Megálos Mourtiás**, **Yiália** and **Megáli Ámmos**.

**The Mediterranean monk seal is severely endangered and very sensitive to human interference, particularly from fishermen. The tiny uninhabited island of Pipéri has been set aside purely for the seals. Visits are strictly for scientists only.**

## Skýros

Southern Skýros is barren and windswept and its northern section wooded and green. The English poet Rupert Brooke died here of an infection in 1915 and is buried at the well-protected bay of **Trís Boúkes**.

The white buildings of **Skýros town** rising up the mountain are beautiful and the village streets, negotiable only on foot, are quite pleasant. Tourism is active along the main street running between the rarely used village square and an idealised statue of Rupert Brooke, but neither the town nor the island ever gets overly crowded. The monastery of **St George of Skýros**, founded in 962, is within the Byzantine built **kástro** above the town; the fortifications were added later by the Venetians.

Skýros beaches that you can get to by car (**Aspoús**, **Péfkos**, **Ághios Fokás**, **Mólos**, **Magaziá**) are good, but the small beaches on the southwest and northwest coasts, accessible by boat from **Linariá**, are wonderful.

# THE NORTHERN AND EASTERN AEGEAN

The Northern and Eastern Aegean Islands are Thásos, Samothráki, Límnos, Lésvos (Mytilíni), Híos, Ikaría and Sámos. Below are descriptions of a few of them.

## Thásos

Only an hour by boat from Kavála, **Thásos** is the northern-most Aegean island, mountainous, covered in pine forests and olive groves, with lovely mountain villages (Panaghía), and miles of beach. It also has the ancient city of **Limínas**, a Hellenistic theatre, a medieval fortress, a temple of Athína, and a shrine to Pan, all behind Limínas. The best beaches are **Parádisos** and **Alykí**.

**A quiet *tavérna*
on Lésvos**

## Samothráki

**Samothráki** is very green and heavily wooded, with abundant water. Boats dock at **Kamariótissa** and the largest village, **Hóra**, is on the slopes of **Mt Fengári**, from the top of which, according to Homer, the gods watched the battle of Troy some 120km (75 miles) to the east. The small **Ághios Andréas lagoon** past the windmills at Kamariótissa is a wetland reserve for many migrating and nesting birds.

Lésvos is famous for its olive trees

The **Sanctuary of the Great Gods** and its very good **museum** (open Tues–Sun 8.30am–3pm; admission fee) are above the small modern village of **Paleópolis**. Here the famous Hellenistic statue, *Victory of Samothrace*, now in the Louvre in Paris, was found in 1863, but you will see remains of the largest ancient Greek **rotunda** (21.6m/65ft in diameter) and the columns of the **Hieron**. The 15th-century Italian rulers, the **Gattelusi**, built the **castle** dominating Hóra and the two **towers**, one at Paleópolis and one at the mouth of the **Foniás River**, which has a fine waterfall. There are lush surroundings and hot springs at **Thermá**. The best beach is **Pahiá Ámmos** on the southern coast.

## Límnos

**Límnos** is an agricultural island not swamped with tourism. Its large bay of **Moúdhros** provided safe anchorage for the ill-fated World War I Gallipoli campaign against Turkey. It has the neolithic site of **Polióhnis** (near **Kamínia**) and the newer sites of **Ifaistía** and beautifully located pre-classical **Kavírio**, all in the eastern part of the island. The main port town is **Mýrina**, on the west coast. The wonderful long beaches of **Platýs**, **Thános** and **Nevgátis** are south of **Mýrina**. The beaches of **Borósokos**, **Platiá Ámmos** and **Aghía Eiríni** are on the east coast and **Ághios Ioánnis** and **Avlónas** are on the west coast north of Mýrina.

## Lésvos (Mytilíni)

**Lésvos**, Greece's third-largest island, after Crete and Evia, is cut by two large bays, **Kallóni** in the centre and **Yéra** to the east. The main port city of **Mytilíni**, below the Byzantine/-Genoese *kastro* (castle) on the headland, is a large

> The poet Sappho is famous for her poems describing love between women. From her great fame in antiquity, it seems this was much more accepted then than in later centuries.

working town. In addition to the **Archaeological Museum** which explains the island's long history clearly, don't miss the two fascinating art museums in **Variá**, 3.5km (2 miles) south, the **Theophilos** and the **Teriade**. Theophilos was a Greek folk painter and Teriade (Eleftheriadis) worked in Paris publishing works by great 20th-century artists.

Vaterá, on the southwest coast below Kallóni Bay, is an 8-km (5-mile) long stretch of beach. The resort area of Plomári, known for its good *oúzo*, is to the south. The beach at Skála Eressoú, on the west coast, is almost as long as the Vaterá beach and almost as popular. Eressós is the birthplace of the ancient Greek poet, Sappho. The **petrified forest** park is between Sigrí and the **Ipsiloú Monastery**. The loveliest town on the island is well-preserved Mólyvos (Méthimna), nestling on the slope beneath the 15th-century Genoese castle.

# THE DODECANESE ISLANDS

*Dhódheka* means 'twelve', but there are more than 150 islands and islets here, 26 of them inhabited. The 12 islands after which the group is named are Astipálea, Kós, Kálymnos, Kárpathos, Kássos, Kastelórizo, Léros, Níssyros, Pátmos, Rhodes, Sými and Tílos. They have been controlled by crusaders, Italians and Ottomans, all of whom left distinctive traces. Here we describe Rhodes, Kós, Níssyros and Pátmos.

## Rhodes

**Rhodes** is fascinating and beautiful. In their effort to save the Holy Land from Islamic rule, the Knights of St John captured the island from the Byzantine Christians in 1308. The Ottoman Turks controlled it from 1522 until Italy invaded in 1912, occupying the island until 1943. Rhodes, and all the Dodecanese, formally became part of Greece in 1948.

Most of the medieval buildings in Rhodes town were erected by the Knights, whose crests can be seen in Ippotón Street, the **Street of the Knights**. You can tour the medieval city walls and visit many of these buildings: the **Palace of the Grand Masters** (open daily 8.30am–9pm in summer, 8.30am–2.30pm

**The Street of the Knights**

in winter; admission fee); the **Knights' Hospital**, now the **archaeological museum** (open daily 8am–7pm in summer, Tues–Sun 8.30am–3pm in winter; admission fee); the **Knights cathedral**, now the **Byzantine museum** (open Tues–Sun 8.30am–3pm; admission fee); the **Turkish** *hammam* (baths) and a number of **mosques**. The town is also dotted with

**Monólithos, Rhodes**

buildings constructed during the Italian occupation, such as the Administration, Theatre, and Naval Administration buildings around **Eleftherías Square** by the port of **Mandhráki** and the **Kallithéa Baths** just outside of Rhodes town.

The site of ancient **Kámiros** 36km (22 miles) south of Rhodes town on the west coast is on gentle slopes near the sea, but by far the most impressive ancient site is the **acropolis of Líndhos**, on the east coast. The village at the foot of the acropolis can get packed with tourists, but it remains beautiful. On the acropolis, inside the powerful defensive walls built by the Knights, are remains of the **Sanctuary of Athena Lindia**, a **stoa,** a **monumental staircase**, a **propylaea**, and a **temple** dating from the late 5th to the 3rd century BC. At the start of the climb is a relief carving of the stern of an ancient oared fighting ship.

The best beaches on Rhodes are on the east coast, less exposed to the prevailing winds. For most of the distance between Rhodes town and Líndhos the beach is one long un-interrupted resort (Faliráki, Kol˘mpia, Ladhikó, Afántou, Tsampíka, Arhángelos, Aghía Agáthi, Maséri, Vlyhá), but the pressures of tourism relax after Líndhos, notably at **Glýstra**.

## Kós

**Kós** has a wonderful architectural mix, proving its turbulent history. The 15th-century **Castle of the Knights** (open Tues–Sun 8.30am–3pm; admission fee) dominates the harbour. Behind the castle is the 18th-century **Hadji Hassan Mosque** with its fountain beside the very large, so-called **plane tree of Hippocrates** (in reality only 500 years old). Ancient Kós is directly south of the castle, and to the south and west of the **agora** are a number of Hellenistic and Roman remains, as well as classical temple foundations. The **old town**, now heavily commercialised, is a wonderful maze of narrow streets and shops. The modern town was largely built by the Italians after a disastrous 1933 earthquake.

> St John the Evangelist was the writer of Revelation (the Apocalypse). Purportedly he had a divine vision in a cave on the island of Pátmos, which he subsequently wrote down, and this now forms the final book of the Bible. The cave is an important pilgrimage site.

The main ancient site on Kós is the **Asklepieion**, a sanctuary dedicated to Asklepios, the god of healing. It owed much of its prestige to the fact that Hippocrates, the greatest physician of antiquity (460–370BC), was born on Kós. The site functioned like a sanatorium, in which the patients dieted and exercised as well as awaited a cure from the god.

Most of the northern coastline is occupied by tourist resorts, starting at well-developed **Tingáki** and **Marmári** and continuing at calmer **Mastihári**. **Kardhámina** on the south coast is extremely developed. The southeastern coast is much quieter and has long stretches of sandy beach, notably between Parádisos and Kamári. **Ághios Stéfanos** has the added advantage of a well-preserved ancient basilica right on the beach. The water at **Bubble Beach** is warmed by volcanic fumes coming up from the seabed.

## Nísyros

Nísyros has an **active volcano** (it last erupted in 1888), with bubbling sulphur pits in its caldera. The island is fertile and so not dependent upon tourism, but many people come on day trips during the summer from Kós and Rhodes. The pretty port town, **Mandhráki**, lies beneath a Venetian **castle**. The massive walls of **Paleókastro (Old Castle)** date back to the 5th century BC. The villages of **Nikiá** and **Emboriós** have wonderful views of the caldera, known as **Lákki**. There are good beaches at **Páli**, on the northern coast.

The Monastery of St John the Theologian, Pátmos

## Pátmos

The main attraction of Pátmos is the impressive **Monastery of St John the Theologian** (open daily 8.30am–1pm, also 4–6pm Sun, Tues, Thur), begun in 1088, and **Monastery of the Apocalypse** (open daily 8am–1pm), begun in 1090 and containing the **Grotto of the Apocalypse**, both above the harbour town of Skála. **Hóra**, the main town, has many early 19th-century houses. Patmos also has many well-protected bays and fine beaches: **Mellí**, **Agriolívadho**, **Kámbos**, **Vághia**, **Livádhi Yeranoú** and **Kakóskala** all on the east coast north of Skála; **Lámbi** on the north coast; and **Psilí Ámmos** on the east coast south of Skála.

# CRETE

**A fishing boat in Sitía's harbour**

Crete is a world unto itself, with mountains, gorges, beaches, Minoan sites, Venetian and Ottoman monuments, and more than 600 Byzantine churches. The Minoan Bronze Age (*circa* 3000–1000BC) peaked just before 1500BC, apparently about the time of the volcanic eruption of Santoríni, but continued after the disaster. Greek-speaking invaders took over the island and it became a backwater until the Roman Empire took over in 67BC. Under Byzantine rule, Slavs, Armenians and Anatolian Greeks settled on the island. The Venetians took control of Crete as a result of the Fourth Crusade in 1204, and a powerful Creto-Venetian culture developed, of which we have a glimpse in the painter Dominikos Theotokopoulos, better known as El Greco. The Ottomans captured Iráklio in 1522 after a 22-year siege, and uprisings against their rule occurred in 1770, 1821 and 1896. In 1898 Crete became largely autonomous, though nominally under Turkish rule, until, in 1913, it became part of Greece.

## Iráklio

**Iráklio** is the island's capital and main harbour. The **Venetian harbour** is protected by the 16th-century **castle**, with a fine Lion of St Mark on its facade, and the **Venetian walls** enclose the old town. The 17th-century **Morosini Fountain**, with its wonderful lions, is in the centre of **Platía Venizélou**, and the church of **St Mark** and the

**Loggia** face the square. The market, on 1866 Street not far from Platía Venizélou, is the city's heart. The 15th-century church of **St Catherine** is in **Platía Aghía Ekateríni**. The **archaeological museum** (open daily 8am–7pm, Mon noon–7pm; admission fee) is west of the market and provides a wonderful chronological presentation of the island's varied life, from 6000BC to the 1st century AD.

## Knossós and Festós

The extensive Minoan remains of the **Palace of Knossós** (open daily 8am–7pm; admission fee) are 5km (3 miles) from Iráklio. It is easy to understand how the complicated site came to be believed as the labyrinth home of the Minotaur. Much of what you see was reconstructed by the archaeologist Sir Arthur Evans, who excavated the site in the early 1900s, and his work is controversial. Nonetheless, the palace complex – grand stairway, throne room, royal apartments, dolphin wall painting, giant storage jars – is impressive indeed.

**Part of Evans' reconstruction at Knossós**

The second major Minoan centre, **Festós** (open daily 8am–7pm; admission fee) is 63km (39 miles) southeast of Iráklio and was a palace as sumptuous as Knossós, but the excavations here have been carried out without reconstructions. The location commands a wonderful view over the **Messara Plain**. The small Minoan palace of **Aghía Triáda** is nearby. **Górtys**, east of Festós, was the capital of both Crete and Cyrenaica in North Africa under Roman rule. The **Law Code of Górtys** is carved into the theatre's long back wall, written from right to left and then from left to right.

## Réthymno

**Réthymno** is dominated by the 16th-century Venetian **Fortezza** (fortress). The harbour area from the Fortezza runs to the east into a wide beach packed with fast-food and tourist shops and innumerable people. The western part of town is quieter and has many Venetian buildings, notably the **Loggia**, the **Rimondi Fountain**, and the church of **St Mary**, still with a minaret from when it served as a mosque.

**Plakiás beach on Crete's south coast**

## Hanía

**Haniá**, dominated by the White Mountains and the sea, consists of one old and one new town. The new surrounds the old and is growing rapidly. The old town, enclosed by 16th-century **Venetian walls**, has its own older section including the inner **Venetian harbour** and extending past the **Kastélli** (citadel). The newer section of the old town is made up of the outer harbour and what were Muslim and Jewish residential areas, including the recently reconstructed **Etz Hayyim Synagogue**. The **Archaeological Museum** (open Tues–Sun 8.30am–3pm; admission fee) is housed in the former Venetian church of **St Francis**. The **waterfront**, filled with shops, cafes and bars, can become packed.

## Ághios Nikólaos

**Ághios Nikólaos** is a highly developed, often expensive, very pretty resort town. Some extremely luxurious resort hotels are at **Eloúnda**, about 11km (7 miles) north of Ághios Nikólaos. The famous beach of **Váï**, on

The incomparable scenery along the famous 14-km (9-mile) Samariá Gorge, a steeply cut ravine through the White Mountains to the sea, is enjoyed by thousands of visitors each year. The walk down takes about 5hrs. Wear good walking shoes, bring water, and do the walk with an organised tour so you will have transport back.

Crete's northeastern corner, with its unique species of palm trees, remains beautiful despite the proliferation of beach chairs and umbrellas. The **Lassíthi Plain**, some 850m (2,500ft) up in the **Dhíkti Mountains**, has thousands of windmills and is well worth seeing, and you may want to visit the **Dhíktian Cave** (open daily, summer 8am–6pm; admission fee), the leading claimant to being the mythological birthplace of Zeus.

## WHAT TO DO

In addition to the wealth of archaeological sites, Greece offers a wonderful coastline and beautiful mountains, with many more attractions in between. If your first choice is for the beaches, you'll find that developed ones can be crowded in high summer because of their facilities and ease of access, but you can always find your way to a less crowded beach off the beaten track.

## WATERSPORTS

**Swimming.** For most summer visitors, the sea is the dominant fact of outdoor life. There are innumerable beaches on the approximately 23,000km (14,000 miles) of coastline and the summer weather is inviting. You can almost always find a sheltered cove or a beach on the lee side of the island.

**Diving.** Scuba diving is a popular sport and there are many diving shops. The Union of Diving Centres (tel: 210 411 8909) can direct you to diving schools and centres.

**Para-gliding, waterskiing.** The larger, more organised beaches have facilities for waterskiing and para-gliding, some of them with waterskiing instruction for children.

**Windsurfing.** If you do want wind, many beaches have it blowing shoreward in steady supply, sometimes quite strongly, so perfect for windsurfing. Many windsurfers descend on Greece from all over Europe to such fine windsurfing beaches as at Vassilikí, on Lefkádha in the Ionian Islands, and at Náousa, on Páros. The Greek Windsurfing Federation (tel: 210 3233 696) can direct you to the best windsurfing schools and beaches.

**Sailing.** Sailing in the Greek islands can be wonderful. Even the Argo-Saronic Gulf islands near Athens have quiet coves and beaches inaccessible by road (or considerably enhanced by being reached by boat), and visiting the more remote islands by boat can be the most beautiful way to see Greece. The winds, notably the northeasterly *meltémi*, can be determinate, either moving you comfortably or keeping you in port for days, sometimes many days on end. Strong winds can blow everywhere, of course, but the Ionian tends to have more benign wind than the open Aegean, notably over the Cyclades, and closer access to island shelter. Several companies provide charters, either bare-boat or with a skipper.

## Spectator Sports

**Soccer:** Greeks are avid soccer fans, and one of the basic things any Greek wants to know about another is what team he or she supports. Long discussions, usually gentle arguments, can develop about the comparative merits of teams, players, coaches and, as often as not, the owners, such as Orestes Kokkalis, an electronics and media tycoon who owns Olympiakos. The 21 major teams are based in the larger cities and competition is intense. Athens has Panathinaikos and AEK, Piraeus has Olympiakos, Thessaloniki has ARIS, and Crete has OFI. When a major game is on, much of the population stops work to watch the TV, and if a team scores it can be heard throughout town.

**Basketball:** Basketball was introduced into Greece as early as 1918, but it was slow to take off. The game was transformed in the 1980s by an American-born Greek named Nick Gallis, who, although less than 6ft tall, had played in the American NBA and seemed to float in the air. He joined Panayiotis Yannakis and Panayiotis Fassoulas (now a member of parliament) to lead the national team to win the European Basketball Championship in 1987, beating Russia in a seesaw final that ended with Greece winning by two points. This display of talent brought widespread popularity and continued results. Greek teams have been in the final four of the European Cup frequently; PAOK won the cup in 1992 ARIS won in 1993, Olympiakos won in 1997. Foreign players, often from the NBA, play with Greek clubs and the Greek game is thriving.

# LAND SPORTS

**Mountain/Rock Climbing.** Most of the country is mountainous, so if you know what you are doing you can spend your entire time in the country mountain climbing. The most spectacular rock climbing is at Metéora, near Kalambáka, where the sheer cliffs are a distinct challenge.

**Skiing.** For all the automatic association Greece has with warm weather, skiing is quite a popular sport here, with ski centres on Mt Parnassós, near Delphi; at

**Windsurfers can benefit from the northeasterly** *meltémi*

Kalávryta in the northern Peloponnese; at Tymfristós, near Karpenísi in Central Greece; at Pertoúli near Kalambáka in the southern Píndhos; in Pílion; and in several centres in Macedonia, including Vassilítsa, near Grevená and Kastoriá. Ski lifts operate at all these centres and you can usually hire the equipment you need.

**Walking/trekking.** After the sea, this is the other great attraction in Greece, because the mountains are extensive, uncluttered and beautiful. The most famous walks are the Samariá Gorge in Crete and the Víkos Gorge in Epirus, roughly 5 and 8hrs respectively. You can, however, take lovely walks all over the country, certainly on the islands and even on Mt Párnitha in Athens. Be sure to take water with you and don proper footwear, and it is a good idea to ask the locals for information before you set out. Several tour companies organise treks and you can also get solid information from the Federation of Greek Excursion Clubs.

# SHOPPING

## What to Buy

A few big chain stores notwithstanding, Greece still is very much a nation of shopkeepers and local producers, meaning small stores of infinite variation are dotted all over the country. Different areas have different specialities. Virtually every area has its own products, especially yoghurt, cheeses and honey. For example: Pýlos in the Peloponnese has *pastéli*, a sweet made with honey and sesame seeds; Messolóngi has *avgotáracho*, dried mullet roe; Aráhova has hand-woven blankets and rugs; Kalamáta and Ámfissa have olives; Kastoriá has furs; Métsovo has hand woven cloth, embroidery and wood carving; Préspes has delicious broad beans; Thessaloníki has Asia Minor sweets (the Hatzí chain of sweet shops); Aegina has pistachios; Santoríni has lentils and wine; Sámos has sweet wine; Híos has mastic, used among other things in chewing gum; Skýros has ceramics and wood carving; Lésvos has *oúzo*; Náxos has *kitron* liqueur; Corfu has jellied kumquat and kumquat liqueur; Sýros has an almond sweet named *amygdalotá*; Kálymos and Sými have sponges; Lefkádha has embroidery and its local salami, cured in the open air and known as *salámi éros*; Haniá has hand-blown glass; several places in Greece, especially Crete, are known for hand-woven cloth.

> **Many good modern Greek artists have their paintings displayed in galleries throughout the country. Silk prints of their work may be available at relatively reasonable prices.**

**Handicrafts.** You will find some good knitted wear, embroidery, and carpets *(kilímia)* in the shopping areas of major towns, but you might find them in the villages where they are made. Jewellery is something of a cottage industry, available in stores all over the country and sometimes of fine quality and originality. Pottery, produced in Greece since antiquity, remains a thriving industry throughout the country, from mass-produced souvenirs to finely made works of art. If you are attracted to antiques or icons, or copies of antiques or icons, be aware that the store knows full well the value of what it is selling. Buy only from established stores, where you will pay high prices but can be assured of quality.

**Greek speciality foods.** There is a wide variety of local cheeses. Greeks are particularly fond of thyme-flavoured honey, but pine-flavoured honey is just as good and more easily available. *Avgotáracho*, sun-dried mullet roe, pressed into rolls and preserved in wax, is a Greek delicacy, best eaten in very thin slices on toast. Some very good *vins d'origine* wines are produced in Greece, particularly in Macedonia and the Peloponnese, but also in Epirus, in Métsovo.

**Dried fruits and nuts in Athens' market**

**Ornamental vase**

## Where to Buy

In Athens, shopping in Plàka, the area below the Acropolis extending down to and below Monastiráki Square, tends to be along Adrianoú Street, lined with shops selling all kinds of tourist tat. If you start at the eastern end of Pandróssou Street near the cathedral and walk toward Monastiráki Square you will find several quality shops selling works of art, jewellery, leather work, rugs and carpets, and one store with comfortable casual wear, sometimes fine heavy-knit sweaters. Below Monastiráki Square on Ifaístou Street the shops are more focused on flea market fare, with shoes, taped music, tools, work clothes and pottery. Near the end of Ifaístou Street is the flea market itself, with stores selling often quite good second-hand furniture and peddlers with goods laid out on the ground – sometimes interesting memorabilia/junk, from old posters and 78rpm records to coins and old farm implements to anything that could be removed from some long gone attic and carried down here for sale. On Sunday morning, the big selling time, Ifaístou Street and Monastiráki Square are full of milling crowds.

The main shopping areas for Athenians are Ermoú Street, now for pedestrians only all the way from Sýntagma Square down to Monastiráki, and the Kolonáki area, where shops are more up-market. In Thessaloníki, the main shopping streets are Tsimiskí, Venizélou, Aghías Sofías, Ermoú, Mitropóleos, Egnatías and Metropolítou Iossíf.

Wherever you are, find the old markets, which usually consist of a food market and an area selling local products, from honey to hand-blown glass. On the islands, these are usually in the centres of the port towns. In Thessaloníki it is the Modhiáno, between Ermoú and Iraklíou streets, in Athens between Athinás and Aiólou streets (enter at Aiólou 81).

# NIGHTLIFE/ENTERTAINMENT

Greek nightlife is active, starting late at night and running into the small hours of the morning. All types of clubs are legion throughout the country. Athens and Thessaloníki have the greatest concentrations, but clubs are in virtually every urban area, emphatically including the islands. There are also rock festivals in the summer, usually held some distance out of the major towns and often running for two or three nights. Festivals of all kinds are held throughout the summer all over the country on both the mainland and the islands; check with the local tourist information office. In Thessaloniki the night scene is along the coast east of the city, in the Ladhádhika area, in Panórama, and at the Mylos and Vilka centres outside the city near the railway station.

Outdoor cinemas in Greece are a great pleasure. The atmosphere is comfortably informal and each has a snack

## Athens' Clubs

The clubs in Athens are scattered throughout the city, notably in the Psirrí area (north of Ermoú Street, just west of Monastiráki Square), in the Gázi area (where Piréos and Ermoú meet), along the coast from Glyfádha and continuing south past Vouliagméni, and to the north, up Kiffisiás Avenue and in Kifissiá. The types of clubs are legion, but if you are in Athens and are interested in good jazz, go to the Half Note in Métz, which brings in excellent foreign musicians.

**Ághios Nikólaos at night, Crete**

bar, some serving drinks as well as sandwiches, potato crisps and other snacks, even more of a pleasure when the cinema has small tables dispersed among the seats. Films are not dubbed in Greece, so you will enjoy them in their original language.

## Greek Folk Dance

The Dora Stratou Greek folk dance theatre in Athens, on the side of Filopáppou Hill facing away from the Acropolis, puts on shows throughout the summer. They work hard to present authentic Greek dances.

## Athens Festival

This is one of the great highlights of Athens. Performances, often of classical music, are at the ancient Herodes Atticus theatre below the Acropolis. Ancient Greek plays in modern Greek are staged at the ancient Epídavros theatre. During the winter a fine programme of classical music is presented at the Athens music hall, the Mégaro Mousikís. For information about all Athens Festival performances, contact the box office at 39 Panepistímiou Street near Sýntagma Square. Also ask

> During the summer the Acropolis is open on the night of the full moon, when the site and the city below are particularly beautiful. This is a rare treat not to be missed.

here for information about the Cultural Olympiad, a series of events leading up to the 2004 Olympic Games.

## CHILDREN

The Greeks love children, are tolerant of their antics, and will take them along at all hours of the night when you think the poor things should be in bed. Don't be surprised, when you are having dinner, to find small children running around the *tavérna* or asleep on chairs while their parents enjoy a convivial meal. Organised activities for children are another matter. In Athens the Children's Museum on Kydhathiníon Street is a fine diversion for small children. For slightly older children (and adults), the Goulandris Museum of Natural History in Kiffisiá is a pleasure. In Thessaloníki the onomatopoeic Tsatsuf 'train' running along the waterfront from the White Tower is great for younger kids. Real trains, such as the one from Vólos to Mt Pílion or the cog railway from Dhiakoftó in the Peloponnese up to Kalávryta provide wonderful excursions. In Athens, even the short ride on the *téléférique* up to the top of Mt Lykavitós is a fine way to show children something different. Most ski resorts have slopes and instructors for children, and most of the organised beaches have playgrounds or activities. The many water parks scattered around the country are usually well equipped, with a variety of slides and playgrounds.

# Calendar of Events

**New Year's Day** Feast Day of Ághios Vassélis (Ol Basil). Before western ideas of Santa Claus became widespread in Greece, this was the traditional day on which gifts were exchanged. Children go from house to house singing the traditional *kálenda*.

**6 January**. Epiphany, celebrating Christ's baptism in the River Jordan. The waters are blessed by a priest throwing a cross, nowadays safely attached to a string for insurance, into the harbour, lake or river, from which it is retrieved by local youths diving into the water.

**7 January**. Feast Day of John the Baptist. Also the day in 1948 when the Dodecanese Islands officially became united with the Greek state.

**25 March**. Feast Day of the Annunciation and Independence Day, the day in 1821 when the Greek revolution broke out against Ottoman rule.

Carnival begins three weeks before the beginning of Lent, celebrated with costumes and parties.

**Clean Monday**. The first day of Lent, is widely observed by flying kites and eating traditional Lenten foods.

**Holy Friday**. On the eve of Holy Friday the bier *(epitáphios)* is paraded around each church neighbourhood with the faithful walking behind with candles.

**Holy Saturday**. At midnight, the presiding priest announces that Christ has risen and passes the flame of life from the altar to the myriad of candles held by worshippers crowded inside and outside the church. Fireworks displays burst into the sky, and smaller fireworks are set off by young boys around the congregation. Carefully protecting their candles, the worshippers head home to break the Lenten fast, usually with *magharétsa*, a soup made from lamb innards.

**Easter Sunday**. Celebrated with family gatherings and lamb on the spit and the competitive cracking of red dyed hard-boiled eggs.

**30 June**. Feast of the Holy Apostles.

**15 August**. The Assumption of the Virgin Mary.

**28 October**. Celebration of the Greek refusal in 1941 to accept Mussolini's ultimatum, triggering Greece's heroic stopping of Italy's invasion.

**25 December**. Christmas Day.

# EATING OUT

In general, Greek food is delicious, fresh and well prepared. Traditionally, a restaurant *(estiatório)* does not have entertainment; it is a place for straightforward eating. *Tavérnes*, open only at night, are more social establishments where customers may spend an entire evening drinking and eating. A *kosmiké tavérna* is a *tavérna* with entertainment and a

**At a *psistariá***

great deal of space; usually more expensive than a regular *tavérna*. A *psistariá* has rotary and flat grills for cooking meats and poultry. Apart from lamb, high quality beef and pork is widely available; filet of beef *(filíto)*, can be excellent.

## Mezédhes and Salads

*Mezédhes* are Greek hors d'oeuvres. They can also be used in combination to make up whole meals. Common *mezédhes* include olives; *tzatziki* (yoghurt dip flavoured with garlic, cucumber and mint); *taramasaláta* (fish-roe paste blended with breadcrumbs); *melitzánasaláta* (aubergine salad); *gígantes* (broad beans in tomato sauce); and *dolmades* (vine leaves stuffed with rice and spices). *Kalamarakia tiganita* are pieces of deep-fried squid; *tiropitika* are small pastry parcels filled with cheese; *keftedes* are small meatballs flavoured with coriander and spices; and *Saganáki* is a slice of cheese coated in breadcrumbs and fried. The standard Greek salad of lettuce, tomato, olives and feta cheese *(horiatiki saláta)* is a fine staple. *Chtapódi saláta* (octopus salad) and *tonnosaláta* (tuna salad) are also popular, as are the various cold salads of boiled greens *(hórta)*.

## Main Courses

*Moussaká* (minced meat, aubergine and tomato with béchamel sauce and a cheese topping) was brought to Greece by refugees from Asia Minor. *Pastítsio* (macaroni and minced meat with béchamel sauce) is just as common. *Kleftiko* is braised lamb with tomatoes and *stifado* is braised beef with onions. Each comes in an earthenware pot that keeps the contents piping hot.

*Horiátiki saláta* (Greek salad)

*Briám* (potatoes, tomatoes and courgettes) and *fasolákia ladherá* (string beans and tomato sauce) are two other casserole dishes that never fail, and *fasoládha* (haricot bean soup) is equally dependable.

Meats grilled on a small skewer are known as *souvláki*, while *yíros* are thin slices of meat cut from a spit and served with salad on pitta bread. *Biftéki*, fried minced meat mixed with bread and spices, is ubiquitous, as is sliced baked veal. *Psaronéfri*, filet of pork, is not quite so common but well worth trying. *Yiouvétsi* is veal, pasta and tomato cooked in a pot. *Soutzoukákia* are rolls of minced meat cooked in tomato sauce. *Youvarlákia* are rolls of minced meat covered in egg-and-lemon sauce *(avgolémono)*. For more unusual foods you may encounter *kokorétsi* (sheep innards wrapped in intestines and grilled over a spit), *myaló* (fried sheep brains, or sheep testicles, known as 'unmentionables' *(amelétita)*. If you are in Greece at Easter, try the spicy *magharítsa*, a soup made from finely chopped lamb innards.

The most common desserts are yoghurt with honey, often with walnuts, and two kinds of *halvá*. *Halvá tis Rínas* is a semolina cake and the compact *halvá tou bakáli*, the grocer's *halvá*, is made of flour, tahini, oil, honey and nuts. Sometimes you will find *galaktoboúreko*, filo pastry filled with custard and soaked in syrup, and *baklavá*, made of crushed nuts in filo pastry with syrup. In the summer, particularly late summer, don't miss the abundant grapes, figs, melon and watermelon.

## Local Dishes

In the mountain areas you will tend to find locally made traditional pasta dishes, often egg noodles shaped into tiny

### Fish Restaurants

These tend to be expensive, but have fresh fish unless winds have kept the boats in harbour. Fish soups *(kakavi)* or shrimp *(garídha)* and prawn *(karavída)* soups are good. Fish sizes vary from the tiny whitebait *(maríthes)* and smelt *(atherína)*, to the larger dentex *(synagrídha)*, swordfish *(xifías)* or grouper *(rofís)*. In between are the smaller red mullet *(barboúni* or *koutsomoúra)* and several breams *(tsipoúra, fagrí, sargós, lithríni)*. Cod *(bakaliáros)*, salted or fresh, as well as *galíos*, a kind of shark, is common. *Loútsos*, like a barracuda, is very good. Grilled octopus *(ktapódhi)* and cuttlefish *(soupiá)* are delicious, and deep fried squid *(kalamarákia)*, usually frozen, is often available. On the islands you will find lobster *(astakós)*, usually boiled, but sometimes cooked with spaghetti. In the mountains the best fish is grilled trout *(péstrofa)*.

squares, a large variety of meat and cheese pies, yoghurt, cheeses and honey. Children can become very fond of spoon sweets, viscous syrup served in a glass of cold water and eaten with a spoon. In winter try *trahanás*, a wonderful soup made usually from cracked wheat with dried milk. If you are more adventurous, try *patsás*, a powerful tripe soup made from cow intestines and feet with much garlic, vinegar and fat, devoutly believed to be a cure-all for hangovers and cold weather. You may find a more benign pleasure in cold weather with *loukoumádhes*, fried balls of batter covered with a honey syrup.

> **Many areas in Greece have local dishes. The best way to spot them is to go carefully through the menu and ask what the strangely named dish is. Don't worry if the menu is in Greek – the waiter should know enough English to give at least something of a description.**

In the Lamía and Pílion area the local dishes are *spétsofai*, fried sausages and pepper, and a bean and red pepper soup. Préspes is justly famous for its wonderful flat white beans, delicious in soups, and its indigenous carp. Several kinds of stuffed cabbage, lettuce or vine leaf dishes are found throughout Macedonia, and you will find other variations virtually all over the mainland and the islands. In Ioánnina several restaurants serve the local speciality called *gástra*, lamb or goat baked very slowly beneath a cast-iron cone covered in coals, and in Ioánnina and the surrounding area you can find wonderful fresh trout. Métsovo has several good cheeses. Thessaloníki is known, in addition to *patsás*, for its seafood, such as fried mussels and cheese, mussels and rice, grilled sardines and stuffed squid, and for its desserts, heavily influenced by Asia Minor.

The islands, of course, have grilled fish and octopus and most produce their own cheeses, but you can find much else. Here are examples from some of the Aegean Islands: Páros, cooked snails and sweet, round, cheese pies; Híos, dried tomatoes, pasta, mastic; Lésvos, salted sardines; Santoríni, very good local fava beans, mock *keftédes* – fried cakes made of tomatoes and herbs – and *skordaliá*, garlic purée based on the local yellow squash instead of on potatoes or bread as elsewhere in the country; Sífnos, local chickpea soup baked in a clay pot and several baked sweets; Ándros, Kímolos, Santoríni, Sífnos, Sérifos, Sýros, Tínos all have locally produced pickled capers. Several Dodecanese islands soak olives, after curing, in the juice of bitter oranges.

In the Ionian Islands there is much influence from Italy, such as *sofrítto*, lightly fried veal with garlic and vinegar; *bourthíto*, a peppered fish stew; *biánco*, white fish stew with garlic; *pastitsáda*, a spicy meat, macaroni and cheese dish. There is also an English influence in Corfu's *tzitzibira*, ginger beer, and liquors and sweets made from kumquats.

**Fish on sale in Thessaloníki**

## What to Drink

The tap water is perfectly good all over the country, but many people order a bottle of spring water from one of the numerous brands available. You will find lots of imported beers, but the new local brand, Mythos, produced by the Boutari company, has cornered a solid share of the market.

Greece produces red, white, rosé, sparkling (Zitsa), sweet wines and champagne (Rhodes). White resinated wine is known as *retsína* and rosé resinated wine is known as *kokkinél retsína*. *Retsína* is usually common fare, but some *retsína* can be quite good, particularly when served very cold. The quality of both red and white Greek wines has improved markedly in recent years, and several areas are known for their wine production. The better-known areas for good wine are Neméa, in the Peloponnese; Imáthia and Macedonia in northern Greece; Kefalloniá; Rhodes; Sámos;

**Enjoying a drink in Ía, Santoríni**

Santoríni and Crete. Wherever you go, ask if there is a local wine and try it. You may be pleasantly surprised.

*Oúzo* is a grape distillate with added aniseed oil. It is made all over the country, but the one from Lésvos is most widely known. If you are on Náxos, try the local variety.

*Tsípouro* is a clear fiery grape distillate similar to *grappa*, known as *tsigoudhiá* in Crete. This, too, is made all over the country, but you will not find it widely available. Ask in traditional local liquor shops.

Various liquors are made – again, in all parts of the country – based on kumquats, for example, in Corfu and on the citron in Náxos.

## To Help You Order...

| | |
|---|---|
| Is there a table available, please? | **Ypárhi éna trapézi eléfthero, parakaló?** |
| I'd like a/some… | **Tha íthela éna, mía/meriká…** |
| The bill, please. | **To logariasmó, parakaló.** |

### Basic Foods

| | |
|---|---|
| **aláti** | salt |
| **avghá** | eggs |
| **féta** | sheeps-milk cheese |
| **kremídhia** | onions |
| **ládhi** | (olive) oil |
| **makarónia** | pasta |
| **marmeládha** | jam |
| **méli** | honey |
| **moustárdha** | mustard |
| **omeléta** | omelette |
| **pipéri** | pepper |
| **psomí** | bread |
| **rýzi** | rice |
| **skórdho** | garlic |
| **tyrí** | cheese |
| **voútyro** | butter |
| **xýdhi** | vinegar |
| **yaoúrti** | yoghurt |
| **záhari** | sugar |

### Mezédhes

| | |
|---|---|
| **andzoúyes** | anchovies |
| **dolmádhes** | stuffed vine-leaves |
| **elyiés** | olives |
| **fáva** | split peas |
| **kolokithákia tighanités** | fried courgettes |

| | | | |
|---|---|---|---|
| loukánika | sausages | katepsighméno | frozen |
| melitzánes tighanités | fried aubergines | marídhes | whitebait |
| | | mýdhia | mussels |
| saghanáki | fried cheese | psári | fish |
| spanakópita | spinach pie | sardhéles | sardines |
| taramosaláta | fish-roe dip | supyés | cuttlefish |
| tyropitákia | cheese pies | xifías | swordfish |
| tzatzíki | yoghurt with garlic | | |

## Fruit and Vegetables

| | |
|---|---|
| angináres | artichokes |
| arakádhes | peas |
| domátes yemistés | stuffed tomatoes |
| fasólia | haricot beans |
| hórta | greens |
| horiátiki | 'Greek salad' |
| kolokithákia | courgettes |
| karpoúzi | watermelon |
| maroúli | lettuce |
| lemóni | lemon |
| patátes (tighanités/ sto fúrno) | potatoes (chips/ roast) |
| piperyés yemistés | stuffed peppers |
| portokáli | orange |
| saláta | salad |
| stafýlia | grapes |
| sýka | figs |
| veríkoka | apricot |

## Meat

| | |
|---|---|
| arní | lamb |
| biftéki | minced meat cake |
| brizóla | chop |
| hirinó | pork |
| keftédhes | meat-balls |
| kotópoulo | chicken |
| kréas | meat |
| moshári | veal/beef |
| sta kárvouna | grilled |
| sto fúrno | roast |
| soutzoukákia | meatballs |
| souvláki | spit-roast |

## Fish

| | |
|---|---|
| bakaliáros | salt cod |
| barboúnia | red mullet |
| frésko | fresh |
| gharídhes | prawns |
| htapódhi | octopus |
| kalamarákia | squid |

# HANDY TRAVEL TIPS

*An A–Z Summary of Practical Information*

# A

## ACCOMMODATION

Hotels have long been classified from Luxury, at the top end, down the alphabet from A to E, but this system is being changed. By the 2004 Olympics all hotels will be classified by stars, but in the meantime you will encounter both systems. Roughly, the equivalents are as follows:

Luxury – 5 stars
A – 4 stars
B – 3 stars
C – 2 stars
D, E – 1 star

No matter what the system, good value for money can be found anywhere along the scale. A Luxury (5-star) hotel is so classified because of the facilities it has, such as conference rooms, swimming pools, sauna, and tennis and basketball courts, which have very little to do with the quality of your room. All C-class (2-star) hotels, for example, are en suite, and some of them are among the most pleasant in the country. D- and E-class (1-star) hotels can be perfectly comfortable and clean, and quite reasonably priced if you are travelling on a tight budget. On the islands, in particular, you will find studio apartments and rooms for rent, with 'rooms' often called out to visitors as they walk off the boat. Some of the room arrangements can be fine, but it is wiser not to commit yourself to more than one night until you have seen the place. Studio apartments also vary, but some can be wonderful deals, particularly in more remote parts of an island.

| | |
|---|---|
| I'd like a single/double room with bath/shower | **Tha íthela éna monó/dhipló dhomátio me bánio/dous** |
| How much per night? | **Póso kostézi to vrádi?** |

## AIRPORT

The Eleftherios Venizelos airport serving Athens is roughly 30km (18 miles) from Sýntagma Square in the centre of the city. For flight information, tel: 210 353 0000. The airport express bus E 95 (24hrs) will take you directly to Sýntagma Square in half an hour with light traffic and more than an hour if the traffic is heavy. Only 21km (13 miles) of the new Athens ring road, Attikí Odhós, has been completed, so you are soon on the regular, often crowded, city road system. You may prefer to take the airport express bus E 94 (6am–midnight) to the last station on the metro line, Ethnikí Ámyna (Ministry of Defence), and ride into town more quickly on the metro. A third airport express bus, E 96 (24hrs), circles around Athens to Karaiskáki Square in Piraeus. The fare for all these buses is €2.90, and the ticket is also valid on the metro. Buy the ticket at the kiosk outside the arrivals hall and validate it in the machine on board the bus. The buses leave approximately every 20 minutes (less frequently during the small hours of the morning). A taxi will take just about the same time as the bus and will cost roughly €23 to take you to Sýntagma Square.

The airport operates two information desks 24hrs a day, one in the southern end, Arrival Hall A (Extra-Schengen arrivals), and the other in the northern end, Arrival Hall B (Intra-Schengen arrivals). If you want more detailed tourist information, the National Greek Tourist Office has an office (open 8am–10pm) in the southern end of the airport (Arrival Hall A, Extra-Schengen arrivals) across from the Kafenio snack bar and the airport's designated meeting point.

| | |
|---|---|
| Where can I get a taxi? | **Pou boróna vró taxí?** |
| How much to central Athens? | **Póso káni yia to kéndro tis Athínas?** |
| Does this bus go to Athens/Thessaloníki? | **Aftó leoforío pói stin Athína/Thessaloníki?** |

# B

## BUDGETING FOR YOUR TRIP

Regular return airfares from New York and London tend to run at around $1,200 and £180 respectively, though of course better deals can be found.

**Accommodation**. The price will vary with the classification of each hotel, its location, when you will be there and the length of your stay, but C-class hotels tend to charge about €130 a night for a double room in full season. Studios, again with variations, usually charge between €60 and €100. Rented rooms will cost less than this.

**Eating out**. A good meal in restaurants and *tavérnes* without frills will probably cost around €20 a person, including half a bottle of house wine, but since ordering in these establishments is à la carte you can easily eat for much less. The upper end can rise to over €140 per person.

**Admission fees**. Charges for the smaller archaeological sites and museums tend to be €2 or €3, with the price rising with the site's importance (expect to pay up to €9 for Delphi and Olympia). For the Acropolis the admission fee is €12, but this includes admission to the five other major archaeological sites in Athens (the ancient Greek Agora, the Theatre of Dionysos, the Kerameikos, the ancient Roman agora and the Temple of Olympian Zeus) as well. Admission to some of the smaller museums and sites is free.

# C

## CAMPING

Campsites are licensed by the Greek National Tourist Organisation, so the best way to find one is to visit one of the GNTO information offices. Camping outside a licensed campsite is illegal. Although there are exceptions, local police usually oblige camper vans to move on at sunset.

| | |
|---|---|
| Is there a campsite near here? | **Ipárhi méros yiá kataskénosi kondá** |
| May we camp here? | **Boroúme na kánoume camping edhó?** |

## CAR HIRE (See also DRIVING)

Both major international and local car-hire companies have offices in the major cities and on the islands. Most of the cars have manual transmission. Chauffeur services are also is available; ask at your hotel for details.

| | |
|---|---|
| I'd like to hire a car tomorrow | **Tha íthela na nikiáso aftokínito ávrio** |
| for one day/a week | **yia mía méra/efdhomádha** |
| Please include full insurance | **Me pléri asfália, parakaló** |

## CLIMATE

The warm Mediterranean climate means that in the lowlands the summer is hot and dry, with clear skies, and the heat often relieved by breezes. Usually the weather is benign, but heat waves have occurred in which the temperature has risen to over 40°C (104°F). The mountain areas are much cooler, with considerable rain. Winters are mild in the lowlands, with rare frost and snow, but the mountains are usually covered with snow. Rain in the lowlands occurs mostly between late September and March.

A seasonal northeasterly wind known as the *meltémi* tends to blow in Greece in July and August. Usually it rises in the late morning and stops at sunset, providing respite from the heat. On occasions, however, it can approach gale-force strength and blow throughout the night, obliging even large ships to remain in harbour. The average monthly temperatures for Athens are below.

| | J | F | M | A | M | J | J | A | S | O | N | D |
|---|---|---|---|---|---|---|---|---|---|---|---|---|
| °C | 10 | 11 | 12 | 16 | 20 | 25 | 28 | 28 | 24 | 20 | 15 | 12 |
| °F | 50 | 52 | 54 | 61 | 68 | 77 | 82 | 82 | 75 | 68 | 60 | 54 |

## CLOTHING

For the summer, wear light clothes. Bring long-sleeved shirts, a hat and sunglasses to protect you from too much sun. You can go to most places, including restaurants and the theatre, in casual clothes. A sweater, and often a windbreaker, may be useful for the evening. Bring good walking shoes. In winter, bring the appropriate clothes for freezing temperatures and snow.

## CRIME AND SAFETY (See also POLICE)

Greece is remarkably free of crime, and most areas are safe to walk, even late at night. Pickpockets, however, have been known to operate on crowded buses, metro trains and the pavements of main city squares. Some petty thieves work in teams, with one of them asking a seemingly innocent question to divert your attention, while another walks off with your unguarded bag. For lost or stolen credit cards, call: American Express tel: 210 339 7250; MasterCard tel: 00800 11887 0303 (toll free); Visa tel: 00800 11638 0304 (toll free); Diners tel: 210 9290 200; Eurocard tel: 210 9503 673.

## CUSTOMS AND ENTRY REQUIREMENTS

Citizens from Australia, Canada, the European Union, Israel, Japan, New Zealand, Norway, Iceland, Switzerland and the USA may enter Greece without a visa and stay for up to three months. Citizens from some South American countries do not need visas either, and EU citizens can enter the country with only their identity cards. If you are from any other country, consult the Greek consulates in your area. When registering at a hotel you will be asked to produce your identification documentation.

| | |
|---|---|
| I have nothing to declare | **Dheného típota na dhilóso** |
| It's for my personal use | **Eínai yia prosopikí mou hrísi** |

# D

## DOMESTIC FLIGHTS

**Olympic Airlines**. This state-owned company is the country's basic carrier, flying to all the airports in Greece as well as to many cities overseas. For the last few years it has earned a reputation for delayed and cancelled flights, but the company is trying to improve service. For reservations and information from anywhere in the country, tel: 801 114 4444 (charge is for local call). If you are in Athens, tel: 210 966 6666.

**Aegean Airlines**. From anywhere in the country, tel: 801 112 0000 (charge is for local call); in Athens tel: 210 99 88 300. This new, privately owned airline is growing well and providing a good service. It now flies to Athens, Thessaloníki, Alexandroúpolis, Haniá (Crete), Iráklio (Crete), Ioánnina, Kavála, Corfu, Lésvos, Mýkonos, Rhodes and Santoríni. The company also flies to Rome and several cities in Germany.

**Hellenic Star**, which began flying in 1998, is the newest privately owned airline in Greece. For reservations, tel: 801 122 2555 (charge is for local call) or 210 061 1881. At the moment, the company flies from Athens to Thessaloniki, Híos, Iráklio and from Thessaloníki to Lésvos and Límnos.

## DRIVING

You need a driving licence issued by an EU country or an international driver's licence. Driving is on the right side of the road. In general, the roads are good. The speed limits are 50km/h (31mph) in urban areas, 80km/h (50mph) outside urban areas, and up to 120km/h (75mph) on the national road. Please bear in mind, however, that some Greek drivers do not adhere to sensible driving principles. They may drive too fast, pass dangerously, run stop signs or red lights, enter a thoroughfare without looking or come around blind curves in the middle of the road. Drive carefully, and expect the unexpected.

On major roads in Greece you will encounter standard international road signs. On smaller roads and in towns you may see the following:

| | |
|---|---|
| Detour | Παράκαψη/**Parákapsi** |
| Parking | Πάρκιγκ/**Párking** |
| No parking | ...απαγορέυεται/...**apagoréfetai** |
| Be careful | Προσοχή/**Prosohí** |
| Bus stop | Στάση λεοφορίο/**Stasí leoforío** |
| Stop | Σταμάτα/**Stamáta** |
| Pedestrians | Για πεζούς/**Yia pezoús** |
| Danger | Κίνδινος, επικίνδινος/**Kíndinos, epikíndinos** |
| No entry | Απαγορέυεται η είσοδος/ **Apagoréfetai i eísodos** |

| | |
|---|---|
| Are we on the right road for...? | **Eímaste sto sostó dhrómo yia...?** |
| Fill the tank please, with (lead free) petrol | **Parakaló, yeméste i dexamení me amólivdhi** |
| My car has broken down | **To aftokínito mou éhi ragisméni** |
| There's been an accident | **Eínai distíhimai** |

# E

## ELECTRICITY

220 volt AC, 50 hertz. Most electrical stores have adaptors for the round two-pin sockets used in Greece.

| | |
|---|---|
| I need a adaptor/ transformer/battery | **Hrízomai éna prosarmostís/ metaschimatistís/sistihía parakaló** |

## EMBASSIES (ATHENS)

**Australia**, Soútsou 37, tel: 210 645 0404
**Canada**, Ioánnis Yennádhiou 4, tel: 210 727 3400
**Ireland**, Vas. Konstantínou 7, tel: 210 723 2771
**South Africa**, Kifissiás 60, tel: 210 610 6645
**United Kingdom**, Ploutárhou 1, tel: 210 723 6211
**United States**, Vas. Sofías 112, tel: 210 727 260

| | |
|---|---|
| Where is the British/ American embassy? | **Pou íne i presvía tis Anglías/ Amerikís?** |

## EMERGENCIES (See also HEALTH AND MEDICAL CARE)

Emergency police assistance, tel: 100. For emergency medical assistance, dial 166. Tourist police, tel: 171. Outside Athens, tel: 210 171. The tourist police speak English and can be extremely helpful. Doctors SOS, tel: 1016. Fire, tel: 199. ELPA roadside assistance, tel: 104. Express Service, tel: 154. Thessaloníki tourist police, tel: 2310 554 871. For pharmacies on duty in Athens and Piraeus, see the last page of the Greek section of the *Herald Tribune* or, wherever you are, check the poster in pharmacy windows that list open pharmacies nearby. For duty pharmacies in Thessaloníki, tel: 107. For duty hospitals in Thessaloníki, tel: 104.

# F

## FERRIES

Most boats for the islands leave from Piraeus, but several leave from Rafina, on the west coast of Attica, and you can make some connections at Lávrio, near Sounion on the southern tip of Attica. In recent years many new ships, some of them quite large and providing quite comfortable accommodation, have been brought into service. The best way to sift through the possibilities is with a travel office.

**Flying Dolphins**. Hellas Flying Dolphins, tel: 210 419 9000. This number is often busy, so call repeatedly without waiting. When you get through, bear with the Greek/English recorded message and Greek advertisements until an attendant comes on the line.

# G

## GAY AND LESBIAN TRAVELLERS

The general attitude is tolerant, and the gay and lesbian community is active. The *Deon Print* magazine, published monthly, has up-to-date information about gay friendly restaurants, bars and nightclubs. See <www.deon.gr> and <www.gaygreece.gr>.

## GETTING THERE

The flight time from London to Athens is approximately 3hrs and 20 minutes. The flight times from New York and Los Angeles to Athens are 10hrs 15 minutes and 18½ hours. Most international scheduled flights land in Athens, but Thessaloniki, Iráklio (in Crete), Rhodes and Corfu also take international scheduled flights. The country has a total of 16 international airports, where charter flights land, and an extensive domestic network of small airports. Olympic Airways flies to all the domestic airports. Aegean Cronus flies to Athens, Thessaloníki, Alexandroúpolis, Haniá, Iráklio, Ioánnina, Kavála, Corfu, Lésvos, Rhodes and Santoríni.

## GUIDES AND TOURS

Many companies organise tours in most parts of the country. Ask at your hotel, a travel agency, or the GNTO office. CHAT Tours and Hermes en Grece organize innumerable tours that you can join through any travel agency.

| | |
|---|---|
| We'd like an English-speaking guide/interpreter | **Tha thélame éna anglófono xenaghós/metafrastí** |

## H

## HEALTH AND MEDICAL CARE (See also EMERGENCIES)

There are medical centres in every town all over the country, so at least emergency help is available. In difficult cases patients are transferred by ambulance or helicopter to the nearest large medical centre. Otherwise, to find a doctor, ask in your hotel or phone your embassy.

| | |
|---|---|
| Where's the nearest (all-night) chemist | **Pou íne to pió kondinó farmakío (dhianihtarívi)** |
| I need a doctor/dentist | **Hrízomai éna iatró/odhondhíatrio** |
| ambulance | **asthenofóro** |
| hospital | **nosokomío** |
| Can you help me please? | **Boríte na me voithísete parakaló?** |
| Where does it hurt? | **Pou ponái?** |
| I have been sunburnt | **éxo apó ton ílio** |
| I have a headache | **éxo ponokéfalo** |
| sore throat | **ponólemo** |
| sunstroke | **ilíasi** |
| fever | **piretós** |
| an upset stomach | **anakaméno stomáhi** |

## HOLIDAYS

1 January. 6 January (Epiphany). Clean Monday, the first day of Lent. 25 March, Independence Day. Good Friday. Easter Sunday. Easter Monday. 1 May. Day of the Holy Spirit (early June). 15 August, The Assumption of the Virgin Mary. 28 October, Óhi (No) Day. 25 December, Christmas. 26 December, Boxing Day.

# K

## KIOSKS

Known as *períptera* (singular: *períptero*) in Greek, these mini wonder-stores seem to be located in most *platías* and on any street corner that might bring custom. Originally, they were licensed only to wounded war veterans, and it may be that the *periptero* owner may be the heir of such a veteran, but the man or woman now minding the store is probably just as healthy as anybody else, except that he or she probably works longer hours. Almost all the *períptera* are privately owned concessions, operated individually or by the family, maybe with one helper to lighten shifts.

*Períptera* sell almost anything portable, mainly newspapers, magazines, sweets and cigarettes, but also batteries, toothbrushes and an increasing array of food, including sandwiches, milk, juices, beer and ice cream. A few *períptera* specialise in selling, for example, only dark glasses in the summer and gloves in the winter, but the ruling principle for the vast majority is to sell as many different items as possible, some spreading their wares in ever-growing circles onto the pavement.

For all the widespread use of mobile phones, *períptera* also still serve as public phones, in almost constant use. Since a *períptero* deals with hundreds of people every day, the individual inside is almost always ready and willing to provide directions or help. If you stay in the area long enough, they will also no doubt be happy to politely correct your Greek.

# L

## LANGUAGE

Greek is spoken throughout the country, but several minority communities speak their ethnic languages as well. Some people along the Bulgarian border also speak Bulgarian; the Pomak community in western Thrace also speaks Pomak, a Southern Slavic language; the Vlach community in the Píndhos Mountains also speaks Vlach, a language derived from Latin; the Turkish community in eastern Thrace and on Kós and Rhodes also speaks Turkish. Many well-educated Greeks speak English, French, German and/or, if they have roots in the east, Arabic and Turkish. English, however, is taught in the public schools and is far and away the most frequently used language of communication between Greeks and foreigners. It is unlikely that you will ever be out of reach of someone who knows enough English to understand what you wish to say.

# M

## MAPS

Maps are widely available in bookshops and tourist shops and even grocers in resort areas. In Athens, look out for the wonderful *Historical Map of Athens*, published by the Ministry of Culture Archaeological Receipts Fund and showing the historical centre of Athens and Pláka. One side shows central Athens, while the other side has a large-scale map of Pláka and the ancient city, with all the monuments colour coded by historical period and identified by number.

## MEDIA

**Radio.** Greek news is broadcast in English every morning at 9am on Flash 96FM. Galaxy at 92FM broadcasts CNN radio news most hours. **Television.** CNN is ubiquitous throughout the country. Most hotels have BBC, Sky and major English, French, German and Italian channels.

Three state television channels, ET1 and NET in Athens and ET3 in Thessaloníki compete with some 10 private channels. All channels seem to broadcast talk shows most of the time, but at night they also show foreign movies, not dubbed.

**Newspapers and Magazines**. Two English-language newspapers are published in Greece: The *International Herald Tribune*, with a section on Greek issues, and the *Athens News*, both widely available in major towns and resort areas. Major English-language magazines and newspapers are widely distributed. The monthly *Inside Out* magazine provides useful practical information about what is going on in Athens, and, sometimes, in Thessaloníki. The bi-monthly *Odyssey* magazine provides solid articles on Greek issues. The *Hellenic Quarterly* is a government-funded review of Greek social, economic, and cultural life.

## MONEY

Since the beginning of 2002 Greece has been using the euro, pronounced *evró*, with 100 cents, called *leptá*. Cash machines (ATMs) are widely available and take a variety of cards (though the most common is Visa). Most establishments accept major credit cards.

| | |
|---|---|
| Can I use this credit card? | **Boró na plelíróso me aftín tin kárta?** |
| I want to change some pounds/dollars | **Tha íthela na alázo merikís líres/meriká dholária** |
| Can you cash a travellers' cheque? | **Borétai na aláksat éna 'travellers cheque'?** |
| Where's the nearest bank? | **Pou íne i trápeza kondá?** |
| Where's the nearest bureau de change? | **Pou íne to tamío yia sinállagma** |
| Is there an ATM nearby? | **Íne to atm kondá?** |
| How much is that? | **Póso káni aftó?** |

## MOVING ON

The least-expensive way to get to Albania, Bulgaria or Turkey is to travel by any one of the frequent buses leaving from the Pelopinissou railway station for points north. For information, ask a Greek speaker to call 210 5298 739. The Pelopónissou railway station is just north of Platía Karaiskáki, which is slightly west of Omónia Square.

**Albania**. Buses leave at 8am and 8.30pm daily for Tirana. Fare €35.20. Avlona, 10pm daily except Thur, €35.20.
Koritsa, 4.30pm and 6pm daily except Tues and Sat, €35.20.

**Bulgaria**. Buses to Sofia leave 7am every day except Mon, arriving at 8pm, one-way fare €45.50. Buses for Plovdiv (Philippopolis), Plevin and Várna leave daily except Thur at 5pm.

**Turkey**. Buses leave daily except Sun at 7pm and arrive in Istanbul at 4pm the following day. The one-way trip costs €67.50; a return trip ticket costs €121.20.

**Trains**. You can travel by train from Athens through Thessaloníki and then on to Eastern and Western Europe or Turkey. For information about trains, ask a Greek speaker to call the train company's central information number, tel: 210 529 7777.

The train from Athens to Istanbul leaves daily at 11.15pm and arrives at 9.30pm the following night. The fare is €62.

## O

## OPENING HOURS

Government offices are open 8am–3pm weekdays, except holidays. Shops are open Monday, Wednesday and Saturday 9am–3pm, and on Tuesday and Saturday from 9am–8pm. Banks are generally open from 8am–2.30pm, but some open again in the evenings, from 5–8pm. Groceries and other shops in resort areas may stay open 9am–10pm, seven days a week. Petrol stations are open from 7am and may stay open until 10pm in the summer. In the major cities petrol stations take turns to remain open all night.

# P

## POLICE (See also CRIME AND SAFETY)

For emergency police assistance, call 100. The tourist police number is 171.

| | |
|---|---|
| Where is the nearest police station | **Pou íne to astinomikó tmíma kondá?** |
| I've lost my wallet/bag/passport | **Éxo hási to portofóli mou/ tin valítsa mou/to dhiavatírio mou** |

## POST OFFICES

Post Offices are open from 8am–2pm. In Athens the post offices in Sýtagma Square at the corner with Mitropóleos Street and off Omónia Square at 100 Aiólou Street have longer hours than this: weekdays from 7.30am–8pm, Sat 7.30am–2pm, Sun 9am–1.30pm.

| | |
|---|---|
| Where is the nearest post office? | **Pou íne to tahidhromío kondá?** |
| stamp | **ghrammatósimo** |

## PUBLIC TRANSPORT

**Taxis** are less expensive than in most other European countries. Rates are set by the State and apply across Greece. The minimum fare is €1.47 and the meter starts at 73 cents. There are additional charges of 15 cents for each bag over 10kg (22lb); 44 cents for ports, railway stations and bus terminals; 88 cents for the airport; 1 euro 17 cents if called by radio; and 38 cents for trips between midnight and 5am.

Radio taxis, Athens: Áris, tel: 210 346 7167. Ermés, tel: 210 411 5200. Enótita, tel: 210 645 9000. Íkaros, tel: 210 515 2800. Kósmos, tel: 210 420 7244. Piraeus I, tel: 210 413 5888.

**Buses.** Extensive networks of buses and trolley buses provide inexpensive transport around Athens, and the new metro is also fast. The basic fare is 70 cents, and the authorities are working to make the same ticket valid on all systems. Public transport operates from 5am until midnight. For questions about Athens public transport, ask a Greek speaker to call 185. For general information about bus routes throughout the country, visit the bus organisation's website, <www.ktel.org>.

From Athens, buses leave for towns in Attica (Lávrio, Sounion, Néa Mákri, Marathon, Rafina, Oropós, Kálamos) from Platía Aigýptou or the adjacent Mavromatéon Street or by the Pedion to Áreos Park, one block east of the junction where Alexándras Avenue and Patíssion meet. One bus also leaves from Platía Aigýptou for Thessaloníki.

The two main bus stations are at 260 Lísion Street and 100 Kifissoú Street. In general, places in the northeast (such as Kateríni, Lamía, Lárisa, Kými) but also in the near northwest (such as Livadiá, Delphi, etc) leave from Lísion Street. Buses for the Peloponnese and northwest Greece (ie, Corfu, Lefkáda, Igoumenítsa) leave from Kifissoú Street, as do buses for Thessaloníki. Both of these terminals are large and busy, with buses leaving and arriving all day and most of the night.

Some of the local bus stations throughout the country are listed below. For specific schedules and prices, ask someone who speaks Greek to telephone for you.

Athens, tel: 210 831 7153 or 210 831 7163
Thessaloníki, tel: 231 051 2121
Lárissa, tel: 241 055 4111
Igoumenítsa, tel: 266 502 2309
Ioánnina, tel: 265 102 6404
Kalambáka, tel: 243 202 2432
Kími, tel: 222 202 2257

Vólos, tel: 242 103 3253
Aidipsós, tel: 222 602 4644
Pátra, tel: 261 062 3884-5
Pýlos, tel: 272 302 2230
Trípolis, tel: 271 024 2086
Messíni, tel: 272 202 2234
Kalamáta, tel: 272 102 3145, 272 102 8581, 272 102 2851
Koróni, tel: 272 502 2231
Kipárissia, tel: 276 102 2260
Iráklio, tel: 281 022 1765
Réthymno, tel: 283 102 2212
Haniá, tel: 283 109 3052 or 283 109 3306
Ághios Nikólaos, tel: 284 102 2234

**Trains.** Inter-city trains travel between Athens and Thessaloníki in
about 6hrs and from Athens to Patras (€10) in 3hrs. The two railway
stations, Pelopónnisou and Lárissis, in Athens are next to each other,
with the Pelopónnisou Station closer to Karaiskáki Square. Trains to
the north run up the east side of the country to Thessaloníki, where
connections can be made with Western and Eastern Europe. The high-
speed inter-city trains reach Thessaloníki from Athens in 5hrs and 40
minutes; a first-class ticket costs €37.40. A slower train (7hrs) leaving every day at 11.15pm can carry your car as well. For information,
have a Greek speaker telephone the central train company information number, tel: 210 529 7777.

All trains to the south, including the high-speed inter-city train to
Pátra (€10, 3hrs) and the narrow-gauge line that goes, slowly, down
as far as Kalamáta in the Peloponnese, leave from the Pelopónnisou
Station. For information, you will need a Greek speaker to call 210
529 8735. If you want to take the beautiful hour-long trip by cog rail-
way from Dhiakoftó up to the mountain town of Kalávryta, get a
Greek speaker to telephone the Dhiakoftó station, tel: 269 104 3206.
The round trip costs €7.

**Metro**. The new Athens metro is a wonderful service, offering fast, cheap travel. The basic fare is 70 cents. The new lines run from Monasteráki east through Sýntagma Square and Evangelismós and then northeast to Ethnikí Ámyna (Ministry of Defence) and from Sepólia southeast through Sýntagma Square and the Acropolis down to Dáfni. You can transfer from both these new lines to the old tram-line running from Kifissiá down to Piraeus. The system runs from 5am until midnight.

| | |
|---|---|
| Where can I get a taxi? | **Pou boró na vró taxí?** |
| How much to…? | **Póso káni yia…?** |
| Where is the bus stop? | **Pou íne i stási leoforíou?** |
| When is the next bus to…? | **Póte fevghí to epómeno leoforíou yia…?** |
| I want a ticket to… return | **Tha íthela éna isitírio yia… epistrofí** |
| Will you tell me where to get off? | **Borítai na mou pétai poúna katévou?** |

# R

## RELIGION

Some 98 percent of the Greek population are Greek Orthodox, but there are small communities of Catholics, Protestants, Muslims and Jews. Many people who come to Greece are particularly interested in seeing the places St Paul visited (Philippi, Thessaloníki, Vería, Athens, Corinth, Rhodes, Crete). Others are interested in Early Christian churches (best seen in Thessaloníki, Athens, Vería, Páros, Crete), and later Byzantine churches (throughout the country). Others are interested in the history of Jewish life in Greece (best seen in Athens, Thessaloníki, Ioánnina, Véria, Hálkis, Tríkkala, Vólos, Corfu, Haniá on Crete, Kós, Lárissa, Rhodes).

**T**

## TELEPHONES

The code for Greece is 30. All telephone numbers in the country have 10 digits. Most kiosks have card-operating telephones and sell telephone cards as well. Since hotels usually impose a surcharge for calls made from your room, using kiosks is less expensive. If you are on a remote island you may find it easier to visit the office of the local telephone company (OTE) to make any overseas calls. Directory inquiries, tel: 131. International operator, tel: 161. International assistance, tel: 169. Mobile phones are widely used throughout the country; you can organise renting one for your stay by calling 210 680 8811 or 210 729 1964.

## TIME ZONE

Greece is in the Eastern European time zone, 2hrs ahead of GMT.

## TIPPING

Although a service charge, by law, is included in restaurant bills, the common practise is to leave 5–10 percent more than the bill for good service. During the Christmas and Easter periods, restaurants are required to add an 18 percent holiday bonus to your bill for the waiters.

Tip porters about 60 cents a bag and maids about 60 cents a day. Taxi drivers usually get tipped by rounding off the fare up to the nearest 50 cents. Hairdressers get 10 percent. Cabin and dining-room stewards and guides on cruises are tipped about €1.80 per day.

## TOILETS

All restaurants and bars have toilet facilities. NB: Always place the toilet paper in the small bin provided; Greek plumbing cannot cope with the paper, which will block the system.

| Where are the toilets? | **Pou íne i toualéttes?** |

## TOURIST INFORMATION

The central information office of the Greek National Tourist Organization (EOT in Greek) is located in Athens at Amerikís 2, between Stádiou and Panepistímiou, tel: 210 331 0565, 210 331 0692. Other GNTO/EOT offices are:

**Northern Greece**

Thessaloníki, Mitropóloes 34, tel: 231 022 2935, 231 026 5507, 231 027 1888

Kavála, Filellínon 5, tel: 251 022 8762, 251 023 1653

Komotíni, Soútzoy 15, tel: 273 107 0995

**Epirus**

Árta, Krystállis Square, tel: 268 107 8551

Ioánnina, Napoléontos Zervá 2, tel: 265 102 5086, 265 103 1456

**Central Greece**

Lárissa, Koumoundoúrou 18, tel: 241 025 0919

Vólos, Ríga Feríou Square, tel: 242 102 3500, 242 103 6233, 242 103 7417

Lamía, Platía Laoú 1, tel: 223 103 0065-6

**Peloponnese**

Pátra, Filopimínos 26, tel: 261 062 1992, 261 062 0353

Kalamáta, Kalamáta Marine Administration, tel: 272 108 6868

Gýthio, Vassiléos Yeorgíou 20, tel: 273 302 4484

**Eastern Mainland and Islands**

Piraeus, Zéa Marina, tel: 210 413 5716, 210 413 5730, 210 322 3111

**Northern Aegean Islands**

Lésvos, Aristárchou 6, tel: 225 104 2511, 225 104 2513

**Eastern Aegean Islands**

Sámos, 25th of March Street 4, tel: 227 302 8582

**Cyclades**

Sýros, Ermoúpolis, Town Hall, tel: 228 108 2375

**Dodecanese Islands**

Rhodes, Archiepiskópou Makáriou and Papágou streets, tel: 224 102 3655, 224 102 3255, 224 102 7466

**Ionian Islands**
Corfu, Zavitsiánou 15, tel: 266 103 7520, 266 103 7639
Kefalloniá, Argostóli, tel: 267 102 2248
**Crete**
Ághios Nikóloas, Marína, tel: 284 108 2384
Iráklio, Xánthoudidou 1, tel: 281 022 6081, 281 022 8225,
281 022 8203
Réthymno, Elefthériou Venizélou, tel: 283 102 9148
Haniá, Kriári 40, tel: 282 109 2943, 282 109 2624

# W

## WEB SITES

<www.gnto.gr> for the Greek National Tourist Information site
<www.ametro.gr> for information about the metro in Athens
<www.ose.gr> for train information and timetables.
<www.ktel.org> for bus information and timetables.
<www.greekferries.gr> for ferry information and timetables
<www.culture.gr> for information on museums and sites

# Y

## YOUTH HOSTELS

Athens: Athens International Youth Hostel, Victor Hugo 16, tel: 210
523 1095 or 210 523 4170. Pangration Athens Youth Hostel, Damários
75, tel: 210 751 9530.
Thessaloníki. Alexándrous Vólou 44, tel: 231 022 5946
Pátra. Iróon Polytéhniou 62, tel: 261 044 7278 or 261 022 2707
Olympia. Praxitélous Kondýli 18, tel: 262 402 5580
Santoríni. Firá, tel: 228 602 2387 or 228 602 3864. Ía, tel: 228 607
1209 or 228 607 1465.
Crete. Iráklio, Výronos 5, tel: 281 028 8281 or 281 022 2947.
Réthymno, Tombázi 45, tel: 283 102 2848.

# Recommended Hotels

The following hotels and other types of accommodation in towns, cities and resorts throughout Greece are listed alphabetically. It is best to reserve well in advance, particularly if you will be visiting in the high season.

Prices normally include breakfast and tax. The symbols are an approximate guide to indicate the price for a double room with bath or shower in the high season. Low season rates can be considerably lower. It is sometimes possible to negotiate special deals or weekend rates

| €€€€ | over 250 euros |
|------|----------------|
| €€€  | 150–250 euros  |
| €€   | 50–150 euros   |
| €    | under 50 euros |

## ATHENS

**Grande Bretagne €€€€** 1 Vassílis Yéorgiou, Sýntagma Square, tel: 210 333 0000 <www.grandebretagne.gr> This just-renovated 5-star hotel on Sýntagma Square is the grand old lady of Athenian hotels, the venue for innumerable political, cultural and social events. Be sure your room faces the street, not the inner courtyard. The GB Corner is a wonderfully comfortable place for meals.

**Acropolis View €€** 10 Webster Street, tel: 210 921 730355. Fine small 3-star hotel on a quiet side street on the eastern slopes of the Acropolis near the Herodes Atticus theatre, with some rooms and a rooftop bar looking up to the Acropolis. 32 rooms.

**Pella Inn €** Ermoú and 1 Karaiskáki, tel 210 321 2229 <www.pella-inn.gr>. Family-run hotel between Monasteráki Square and the Thission metro. Basic, clean, friendly. The upper floors facing Ermoú Street have a view of the agora and the Acropolis.

**Hostel Aphrodite €** 12 Einárdou Street, tel: 210 881 0589 <www.hostelaphrodite.com>. Just refurbished, clean, unpretentious, friendly, this small E-class hotel offers a good deal. Slightly off the beaten track but conveniently located for the tram station in Victoria Square. All rooms are air-conditioned, but not en suite. The hostel provides internet services and travel services for guests. Pleasant basement bar, free luggage storage.

**Student Travellers' Inn €** 16 Kydathínion, Pláka, tel: 210 324 4808. Run by the same management as the Hostel Aphrodite. Double rooms are slightly more expensive, but there are dormitory rooms as well (probably the cheapest good accommodation in the city).

## CENTRAL GREECE

# VÓLOS

**Galaxy €€** 3 Aghíou Nikoláou, Vólos, tel: 242 102 0750. Comfortable C-class hotel on a pedestrian street in the centre of town and facing the shore. Rooms at the front have a view over the water towards Mt Pílion, all rooms have air-conditioning and TV. Continental breakfast of orange juice, toast, cheese and cake.

## MAKRYNÍTSA

**Archontikó Karamarlí €€** Makrynítsa, tel: 242 809 9570. Restored late 18th-century stone mansion belonging to the Karamarlí family, with two subsidiary buildings also housing bedrooms. The rooms are heavily decorated in a variety of styles, from Byzantine to art deco; many of them have murals. The rooms are a little small, but the suites more comfortable. Fine views of the sea from the terraces. Good breakfast, excellent service.

## MELÍNA

**Houses of Pelion €€** Melína, tel: 242 306 5471 <www.pelion. co.uk>. Tim and Aphroula Smart have rooms available in several private villas in the southwest of the peninsula, most of them near the water. They can arrange bookings in the beautiful Lost Unicorn hotel in Tsangarada and in the small Old Silk Store bed and breakfast in Mouréssi. They also provide useful services, such as car hire, transfers and hotel reservations elsewhere.

# METÉORA

**Kastráki II €€** Kastráki, tel: 243 207 5336. 1.5km from Kalambá-ka. Small hotel in village between Kalambáka and Metéora. Traditional, wooden building finished in 1995, with pine trees on one side and roses in front. The rooms are simple and clean, with wooden furniture. Half of the rooms have wonderful views toward Metéora, and all are well appointed. The buffet breakfast is abundant.

# DELPHI

**Xenia €€€** Delphi, tel: 226 508 2151/2. Recently renovated, with wonderful views down over the olive groves below towards the sea at Itea. The rooms are light coloured with original paintings on the walls. The bathrooms are clad in pink and white granite. Pine trees surround the garden, some of them close to the swimming pool to provide shade. This is a beautiful, peaceful place.

# GALAXÍDHI

**Galaxídhi €/€€** 11 Sýngrou Street, tel: 226 504 1850. Pleasant, unpretentious, quiet two-storey C-class hotel at the edge of town about 100m (330 ft) from the port. The rooms are fitted with either a double or twin beds, but some are a little small. All have TV, refrigerator, bar, air-conditioning and a small balcony. The garden at the rear is a particularly pleasant place for breakfast, for it is surrounded by flowers and kept cool by a wooden roof covered in tiles.

## EPIRUS

# PÁRGA

**Lichnos Beach Hotel €€** Párga, tel: 268 403 1257 <www.lichnos-beach.com> This very pleasant large hotel 3km (2 miles) from Párga is a haven, with rooms and bungalows in a lemon grove. Family rooms have a bedroom and living room with two sofabeds. The large swimming pool has a section for children and there is a playground by the beach. A shuttle bus (€1) runs between the hotel and Párga.

## IOÁNNINA

**Olympic €€** 2 Melanídhi, tel: 265 102 2233 <www.hotelolymp.gr>. Recently renovated hotel in the heart of town. All the rooms are well appointed, and the newly added fifth floor has slightly larger rooms and more luxurious accommodation, plus a fine view over the lake and mountains. The small Plaza Restaurant serves mostly grilled food but also Italian dishes.

## MEGÁLO PÁPINGO

**Papaevangílou €€** Tel: 265 304 1135. Yorgos and Markella, both from Pápingo, run this handsome hotel built in a local style. Pleasant rooms and a common room with a warm atmosphere and comfortable space where you can eat the delicious homemade breakfast. There are fabulous views of Mt Gamílla.

**Saxonis Traditional Hotel €€** Tel: 265 304 1615. This friendly, quiet hotel is unobtrusively set into the traditional village, its three buildings made of local stone. The large rooms are simply and beautifully designed. Lovely garden, and small terrace for eating breakfast in warm weather. Breakfast is simple but delicious.

## MÉTSOVO

**Victoria Hotel €€** Tel: 265 604 1771. <www.victoriahotel.gr> Very friendly family-run hotel built in the traditional Métsovo style of stone with wooden interiors. The comfortable rooms have a fine view over the mountain. The swimming pool has a hexagonal extension for children. The restaurant on the ground floor serves local dishes: various cheese, meat and vegetable pies, *keftédes*, the local cheese, *metsovóna*, and the good local wine, Katoyi.

## NYMPHÍO

**La Moara €€** tel: 238 603 1377. Small, luxurious hotel built in the traditional style on the slopes of Mt Vítsi. All rooms have fine views over the garden, village and mountain. Abundant, fresh breakfast. A perfect place to stay when visiting the nearby bear sanctuary.

## VÉRIA

**Makedonía €€** 50 Kontoyeorgáki Street, tel: 233 106 6902. The ground and first floors have been renovated, otherwise the hotel is a slightly dated but still quite comfortable B-class hotel, and most of its clientele are visiting businessmen. It is particularly convenient because it is right on the on the edge of Véria, above and to the left of the main road heading north.

## MACEDONIA AND THRACE

## HALKIDIKÍ

**Athos Palace €€€** Kallithea, tel: 237 402 2100.
**Pallini Beach €€€** Kallithea, tel: 237 402 2100.
Two 5-star hotels halfway down the Kassándra peninsula sharing a guard-posted entrance and a long beach of pure white sand. In addition, they have their own swimming pools, shopping concourse, cinemas, snack bars and wooded gardens.
**Xenia €€** Ouranoúpolis, tel: 237 707 1412. Comfortable, beautifully located 4-star hotel right on the sea among olive trees. The main building and bungalows look out over the beach. As well as having the beautiful sea at hand, there is a saltwater pool. Buffet breakfast and dinner. The Mt Áthos monasteries are just down the peninsula.

## KAVÁLA

**Tosca Beach €€** Palió, 6km (4 miles) from Kavála on the Kavála–Thessaloníki road, tel: 251 024 4765. Excellent hotel, renovated in 1999, on private beach beneath pine trees. All rooms have a small balcony.

## THESSALONÍKI

**Makedonia Palace Hotel €€€€** 2 Megálou Alexándrou Avenue, tel: 231 089 7197. This is the grand old lady of Thessaloníki hotels. The location is perfect, on the sea within walking distance of the White Tower. The rooms are large and comfortable, and half have wonderful views over the sea. The Porphyra Restaurant serves fine French food, and the ninth floor bar has a wonderful view.

**Telioni €€** 16 Aghíou Dimitríou, tel: 231 052 7825. Friendly, recently renovated B-class hotel in the old city conveniently near the market and the Ladádika area. This is a fine place to stay for one or two days in the city centre. Buffet breakfast.

## XÁNTHI

**Helena €€** Stratoú Avenue and Panyís Tsaldári Street, tel: 254 106 3901. New hotel by the Kósynthos River, looking towards the mountains and only a short walk to the old city. The rooms are a bit plain but quite comfortable. The staff are pleasant and helpful.

# THE PELOPONNESE

## NÁFPLIO

**Nafplia Palace €€€€** Akronafplía, tel: 275 222 8981 <www.helioshotels.gr>. This fine 5-star hotel is in a wonderful location above the city, within the old Venetian fortifications. Recently renovated, it has large rooms, most of them with fine views down over the bay and the Boútzi. The Amimoni Restaurant is excellent.

**Byron €€** 2 Plátonos, tel: 275 202 2351. Beautiful early 19th-century home, now a small hotel facing the church of Ághios Spyrídon. The antique-decorated rooms are simple and on the small side; the corner rooms have small balconies with views over the city.

## LEONÍDHI (VICINITY)

**Hotel Dionysos €** Pláka, tel: 275 702 3455. This clean, simple hotel enjoys a lovely position right on the beach. It's situated at the edge of a small plain, squeezed into an opening in the mountains.

## MONEMVÁSIA

**Ano Malvasia €€** Old town, tel: 273 206 1323. This hotel's rooms are dotted about the southeastern corner of this walled Byzantine town. Many of them are individual medieval houses, reached down cobbled and vaulted lanes. Most also have terraces, tiny gardens or balconies; some overlook the sea. All have modern bathrooms.

## THE MÁNI

**Tsitsiris Castle €€** In the village of Stavrí, near Yeroliména, tel: 277 305 6297. An old Máni tower, extended and converted into an attractive hotel with views over the olive groves and distant hills and villages. A place with character.

**Akroyiali €** Yeroliména, tel: 273 305 4204. This hotel is a plain, clean concrete structure. All the rooms have been refurbished, and an old stone tower house next door is now part of the hotel. The restaurant (with terrace overlooking the harbour) is as good as any in town.

## METHÓNI

**Castello €** Methóni, tel: 272 303 1300. A clean, simple, modern hotel with a lovely little garden. The rooms are bright and the atmosphere welcoming. It is family-run, and guests are made to feel at home. Close to the beach and the magnificent Venetian castle.

## OLYMPIA

**Olympia Palace €€/€€€** Praxitélous and Kondýli streets, tel: 262 402 3101. A large, completely renovated, luxurious A-class hotel, with lots of marble and glass; all rooms have internet terminals.

## ARGO-SARONIC GULF ISLANDS

## AEGINA

**Plaza €** 3 Kazantzáki Paralía, Aegina Town, tel: 229 702 5600. E-class hotel across from the ferryboat landing. The same management also has two other E-class hotels: the Ulrica and Christina.

**Danae €€** 43 Kazantzáki, Aegina Town, tel: 229 702 2424 <www.danaehotel.gr>. Newly renovated B-class family hotel 700m (2,300 ft) from harbour on a bluff overlooking the sea.

## PÓROS

**Epta Adelfia €** 1 Tombázi, Platía Iroön, tel: 229 802 3412. Family-run C-class hotel in town near the harbour. The rooms are a little small, but the place is well cared for and the management helpful.

**Pavlou €€** Neórion, tel: 229 802 2734. Pleasant, family-run hotel, 2km (1¼ miles) from town, by the water. Half the rooms look over the swimming pool and woods, the others over the water.

## ÍDHRA

**Orloff €€** 9 Rafalía, tel: 229 805 2564 <www.orloff.gr>. Renovated old island mansion, now an attractive A-class hotel. Rooms have air-conditioning. Generous buffet breakfast served in the pleasant garden.

## SPÉTSES

**Villa Martha €€** tel: 229 807 2147 <www.villamartha.gr> This unpretentious but very attractive hotel, southeast of the Old Harbour, is set among trees and flowers. Continental breakfast served in the garden, and there is a minibus transfer to the harbour.

# THE IONIAN ISLANDS

## CORFU

**Cavaliéri €€** 4 Kapodistríou Street, tel: 266 103 9041. Pleasant, recently renovated, well-run A-class hotel on the esplanade *(spianáda)*. The roof terrace has a beautiful view over the town.

**Ermones Beach Hotel €€€** Érmones, tel: 266 109 4241. Large hotel on a wooded hillside with a cable-car down to the small private beach. Rooms are large and fully equipped. Full board.

## LEFKÁDHA

**Nirikos €€** Lefkádha Town, tel: 264 502 4132. C-class hotel at the entrance to town from the causeway. The rooms are large and have air-conditioning. Continental buffet breakfast.

## ITHACA (ITHÁKI)

**Captain Apartments €/€€** Kióni, tel: 267 403 1481 <www.-captains-apartments.gr>. Two-person apartments and four-person studios, with kitchens. On the top of the hill overlooking the sea.

## KEFALLONIÁ

**Lara €€** Lourdháta, tel: 267 103 1157. Wonderful, quiet, family-run hotel, 280m (920 ft) from beach. Rooms have small refrigerators.
**Filoxenia €€** Fiskárdho, tel: 267 404 1410. A 19th-century house beautifully refurbished as a small hotel in the most picturesque village on the island. Right by the water. 6 large apartments.

## ZÁKYNTHOS

**Louis Plagos Beach €€€** Tragáki-Amboúla, 6km (4 miles) north-west of Zákynthos, tel: 269 506 2800. Arguably the most beautiful hotel on the island, surrounded by gardens and right on the beach.

## KYTHIRA

**Vassilis Bungalows €€€€** Kapsáli, tel: 273 603 1125. 12 self-catering studios in an olive grove 200m (660 ft) from the beach.

## THE CYCLADES ISLANDS

## ÁNDROS

**Pigí Sárisa €€** Apíkia, tel: 228 202 3799. Luxurious hotel built in island style in the hillside village of Apíkia, almost on top of the famous Sarisa spring. Restaurant with beautiful views.

## MYKONOS

**Kivotos Clubhotel €€€€** Órnos Beach, tel: 228 902 4094 <www.kivotosclubclubhotel.gr>. Luxury hotel around a pool overlooking the sea. Individually styled rooms. Excellent service and restaurant.

## NÁXOS

**Chateau Zevgóli €€** tel: 228 502 6123 or 6131 <www.naxos townhotels.com>. A small B-class hotel in Naxos old town, near the Glezou tower. Traditional Cycladic architecture and decoration.

## PÁROS

**Pandrósos €€** Parikía, tel: 228 402 2903. Comfortable hotel close to the heart of town and only 100m (330 ft) from the beach, set on a small hill with impressive sea views. All rooms have small balconies.

## SANTORÍNI (THÍRA)

**Atlantis €€€** Fíra, tel: 228 602 2232. This A-class hotel has a wonderful location near the cliff edge, with stunning views over the caldera. All rooms have air-conditioning, and there is a pool.

## SPORADES ISLANDS

## SKÍATHOS

**Atrium €€€** Plátanias, tel: 242 704 9345. Casually elegant hotel, built in traditional style, among pine trees and by a wonderful sand beach. All rooms have air-conditioning and sea views.

## SKÓPELOS

**Adrina Beach €€** Panórmos, tel: 242 402 3371. A-class hotel set on a slope among pine trees. All rooms have air-conditioning and a fine view over the water. Pleasant restaurant specialising in fish and lobster is by the swimming pool above the private beach.

## THE NORTHERN AND EASTERN AEGEAN

**Makryammos €€** 2km (1¼ miles) from Thásos, tel: 259 302 2101. Large hotel complex set among pine trees with private bungalows, on beautiful private beach. Swimming pool and water sports.

## LÍMNOS

**Porto Myrina Palace €€€** Livadohóri, tel: 225 402 4805/6. Large luxury-class hotel on the beach. Outdoor freshwater swimming pools.

## LÉSVOS

**Aeolian Village €€€** Skála Eressoú, tel: 227 305 3585. Large, well-designed resort hotel on Eressós beach on the island's west coast. The large rooms have a balcony or terrace.

## MÓLYVOS

**Pansélinos €€** tel: 225 307 1905–7. Roomy studios and apartments with kitchens, so that you can self-cater. Swimming pool and children's playground. Perfect for families with small children.

# DODECANESE

## RHODES

**Andreas €€** 6 Konstantópedos Street, Rhodes town, tel: 224 102 8489 <www.hotelandreas.com>. Small *pension* in the old town, with great views from the glass-enclosed terrace. All rooms are beautifully designed and feature individual paintings.
**Hotel Isole €/€€** 75 Evdóxou Street, Rhodes town, tel: 224 102 0682 <www.hotelisole.com>. Small A-class *pension* in the heart of the old town. The rooms are quite comfortable and have fine views.

# CRETE

**Elounda Beach Hotel €€€€** Eloúnda, Ághios Nikólaos, tel: 284 104 1412. This extremely luxurious resort hotel on the beach provides the ultimate in self indulgence, with outdoor heated saltwater swimming pool, and helicopter and Learjet services.
**Doma €€** 124 Eleftheríou Venizélou Street, Haniá, tel: 282 105 1772. Neoclassical house 11km (7 miles) from the harbour, overlooking the water. Some rooms have views over a pleasant garden.

## Recommended Restaurants

Remember that local people eat late, and if you arrive just after the restaurants have opened foreign visitors are likely to be the only diners. Reservations are recommended for the more expensive places.

The following symbols give some idea of the average cost of a meal for two, excluding drinks.

€€€ 30–45 euros
€€ 15–30 euros
€ under 15 euros

## ATHENS

**Strofí €€** Pítrou Gálli, Makriyánni, tel: 210 921 4130. Classical Greek *tavérna* serving good food; up narrow stairs on roof terrace with wonderful view up towards the Acropolis.

**To Kafeneio €€** 26 Loukianoú Street, Kolonáki, tel: 210 722 9056. Fashionable, very good restaurant, with a few tables also set outside on the pavement. Fine Greek food, good wines, polite service.

**To Kíoupi €** Kolonáki Square, tel: 210 361 4033. Pleasant basement restaurant that is the open secret for many who live or work in the area. The original stone walls are attractive. You choose the standard Greek food, already prepared, from the kitchen. Good house *retsína*.

**Taki 13 €€** Taki 13, Psyrrí, tel: 210 325 4707. This restaurant is in an attractively refurbished small old house; offers a variety of well-prepared Greek food. Live music. Can be packed on weekends.

**Dourámbeis €€** Aktí Protopsálti 27, Mikrolímeno, Piraeus, tel: 210 412 2092. Best-known fish *tavérna* in Turkolímino, slightly away from the harbour towards Athens. No frills. The fresh fish is well prepared; wonderful crayfish soup and delicious salads.

**Cavouri €€** Marathon, tel: 229 405 5234. The Cavouri fish *tavérna* is about an hour from Athens, right on the water. If you are visiting ancient Marathon, this is a great place for lunch or dinner. The fish is excellent, not over-cooked, and the *taramasaláta* is incomparable.

## CENTRAL GREECE

### MILIÉS

**The Old Station €** tel: 242 308 6425. The last stop on the Vólos to Pílion railway line houses a good mountain restaurant – casserole meat dishes, sausages, wonderful *píttes* – shaded by huge plane trees.

### MELÍNA

**The Penguin €** tel: 242 306 5518. Unpretentious, pleasant fish *tavérna* between the (quiet) road and the sea. The fish are fresh, and the cooking over the grill excellent.

### METÉORA

**Ziógas €** Near Hotel Kastráki, near Kalambáka, tel: 243 202 2286. A popular, long-standing *tavérna*, re-housed in a new building of local stone and wood. Delicious grilled meats and home-made sausage, with wonderful fresh salads.

### GALAXÍDHI

Two of the simplest and most pleasant places to eat are at the end of the harbour towards the Galaxídhi Hotel, **To Stéki €** before the periptero and **To Pórto €** just across the narrow street. **Tássos €€**, just past To Porto, is a good fish *tavérna*.

## EPIRUS

### IOÁNNINA

**The Gastra €** Kostáki 10, tel: 265 106 1530, past the airport shortly before the turn for Igoumenítsa. *Gástra* is a traditional Epirot meat dish baked slowly in a cast-iron dish tightly covered with a lid.
The island in Lake Pamvótis has four restaurants (all **€**) by the landing and two more inland; all are thoroughly pleasant and serve fresh trout and eel beneath large plane trees.

## ZAGÓRIA

**Voidomátis Riverside Tavérna** € On the left bank of the River Aoös Valley not far from the Ioánnina–Kónitsa road. Family run *tavérna* with delicious fresh grilled trout. Tables by the river.

**Tsoumanis** € Megálo Pápingo, tel: 265 304 1893. Extensive menu and warm, welcoming atmosphere; the veranda has a wonderful view. Good grilled meat and chicken, some pasta and casserole dishes, *hórta* (Greek greens), fine *píttes* and salads.

**Dias Restaurant** €€ Mikró Pápingo, tel: 265 304 1257. The best food in the area. Grilled meats, beef *kokkinistó* casserole, pork *lemonáto*, *hórta* and several pies, plus delicious soups. Polite service.

## MÉTSOVO

**Galaxias** € On the square, tel: 265 604 1123. One large room with a wooden-beamed roof. Unsophisticated, with grilled meats, some local casseroles and oven dishes, and various *píttes* (often quite good).

# MACEDONIA AND THRACE

## HALKIKIDÍ

**Tákis** €€ Skála Foúrkas, Kassándra, delicious grilled fresh fish, prawns, and other dishes such as mussels and rice and sea urchin salad, served at tables on the beach right by the water.

## KASTORIÁ

**Krátergo** € tel: 246 702 9981. Krátergo occupies an old two-storey prison on the lake and serves a wonderful array of *mezédhes* that can expand to casserole dishes and grilled meat, supported by salads.

## PRÉSPA

Here, there are very few places to eat, other than meat restaurants in Ághios Yermanós and fish *tavérnas* in Psarádhes. All are inexpensive. In Mikrolímni, try the fish *tavérna* by the small roundabout.

## NYMPHÍO

**Arhontikó €** In the lower section of the village, tel: 238 603 1107. Good grilled meats, including beef, lamb and *kokkorétsi*. Also meats are cooked in clay pots *(stámna)*; also does salads and cheeses.

## THESSALONÍKI

**Krikelas €€** Ethnikís Antistáthios 32, Ladhádhika, tel: 231 045 1289. Long-famous traditional Greek restaurant serving good food, including game. Extensive wine list, courteous service.

**Ta Kioúpia €€** 3–5 Morihoúvou Square, Ladhádhika, tel: 231 055 3239. Pleasant and comfortable, serving a wide range of traditional Greek dishes. In the winter, try the delicious peasant's *trahanás*.

**Hamódrakas €€** 13 M Gagíli Street, Néa Kríni, tel: 231 044 7943. Established by Greek refugees from Asia Minor. Lovely fresh fish, and good shrimps, mussels and grilled octopus. Polite service.

## VÉRIA

**Kóstalar €** tel: 233 106 1801. In Papákia Square, approximately 100m (330 ft) past St Paul's Shrine. Serves northern traditional dishes, largely casserole meat dishes and cheeses. Friendly atmosphere.

## XÁNTHI

**To Ktíma €** 4km (2½ miles) outside town on the Xánthi–Komotiní road, tel: 254 102 1010. Good Greek cooking; oven-baked lamb or pork, seafood, fresh vegetables and salads, with a variety of cheeses. For Anatolian food try **Gonía** and **Fanarákia**, near the National Bank building, **Kípos**, near the river, and **Eródios**, in the old town.

## PELOPONNESE

## ÍSTHMIA, NEAR CORINTH

**I Dióriga €** Eastern end of Corinth canal. Good but nothing special except for the great location on a veranda down by the canal.

## NÁFPLIO

**Ellas** € Sýntagma Square, tel: 275 202 7278. With its old-style wooden tables, this restaurant seems right out of the 1950s, but it serves good-standard Greek casserole dishes at reasonable prices.
**Kanáris** € 1 Bouboulínas, tel: 752 022 7688. Very good traditional cooking – a favourite restaurant of the late Kostantínos Karamanlís. Fine stuffed cabbage leaves and courgette, and a wonderful fish soup.

## MONEMVÁSIA

**Matoúla** € Old Town, tel: 273 206 1660. Eat on the flowery terrace looking over the sea or in the attractive old wooden-ceilinged cafe. The food, notably *dolmades* and *soutzoudákia*, is excellent.

## ARGO-SARONIC GULF ISLANDS

## AEGINA

**Psarotavérna Agora** € tel: 229 702 7308. This is a small *tavérna* for the working man, right behind the fish market. Basic, unpretentious, inexpensive and with very good fresh for seafood.
**Ippókambos** €€ near the old prison. Excellent *mezédhes*. Try the seafood-and-rice-stuffed cuttlefish or baked potatoes packed with pieces of whitefish and shrimp, then have a wonderful fish soup. There are also several good fish *tavérnes* along Pérdhika's harbour.

## ÍDHRA

**Kserí Eliá** € tel: 229 805 2886. Traditional Greek *tavérna* in an old stone Hydriote house with tables in the pleasant square beneath a shaded trellis. Traditional casserole cooking, good *mezédhes*.

## SPÉTSES

**Pátralis** €€ In Kounoupítsa on the right-hand side just past the Spétses Hotel. A verandah suspended over the water. If good fish is available, it will be here, grilled perfectly and never cooked dry.

**Trechandíria** €€ Old Harbour, tel: 229 802 9413. A wonderful setting overlooking the water. Has an Italian slant *(osso bucco)* but Greek enough to have baked kid. Good Greek wine list and polite service.

## IONIAN ISLANDS

## CORFU

**Trypas** €€ tel: 266 105 6333. In the village of Kynopiástes, just south of Corfu town. Quite highly priced fixed menu but an endless flow of very good food arrives at your table without your ordering.
**Roúla** €€ Kontókali, tel: 266 309 1832. Locally famous, pleasant restaurant by the water. It has lobster, seafood and good fresh fish.

## LEFKÁDA

**Regánto** € Off the main square, tel: 264 502 2855. Idiosyncratic with tables set outside. Grilled meats and chicken, fine *pastítsio*, cheese pies, and good *lahanópitta*. Particularly good grilled fish.

## ITHÁKI

**Gregory's** € Just outside Vathý on the northeast side of the bay, in a romantic setting under the trees. Does good meat and fish.
**Kalypsó** € Kióni, tel: 267 403 1066. In a pretty marina, this small *tavérna* serves grilled meats and good fresh fish as well as some casserole dishes. Interesting *pítte* made of cod and rice.

## KEFALLONIÁ

**Kyaní Aktí** € 1 Metáxa Street, Argostóli, tel: 267 102 6680. Beautiful *tavérna* with tables overlooking the water. Delicious, fresh, grilled and baked fish; wonderful *mezédhes*.

## ZÁKYNTHOS

**O Adelfós tou Kósta** €/€€ Zákynthos–Vassilikós road, tel: 269 503 5347. Traditional *tavérna* with fine food; traditional songs sung.

## KYTHIRA

**Ydhraghoghío** (Aqueduct) **€** Above the port at Kapsáli, tel: 273 603 1065. Small *tavérna* on a large terrace with a wonderful view. Delicious *mezédhes* and properly cooked fresh fish. Very good service.

## THE CYCLADES

## ÁNDROS

**Yiannoúlis €** Just outside Gávrio, on beautiful beach, tel: 228 207 1385. Fine casserole dishes, beef *lemonáto* and an interesting chicken and spaghetti dish with tomato sauce.

## MÍLOS

**Aragósta €€** Adámantas, tel: 228 702 2292. A large verandah with of beautiful view. Italian/Greek dishes, a variety of pastas, wonderful seafood, notably lobster, and fine salads. Prompt, polite service.

## NÁXOS

**Nikos Fish Restaurant €/€€** Hóra, on the far left of the harbour as you face the sea, tel: 228 502 3153 or 228 502 3472. Fresh fish is grilled well at this unpretentious *tavérna*.

## SANTORÍNI (THÍRA)

**Tavérna Katína €/€€** Ammoúdhi, on the right at the bottom of the steps from Ía. One of the best on the island. Fresh grilled fish and prawns and local specialities. Friendly service. Summer only.

## THE NORTHERN AND EASTERN AEGEAN

## LÍMNOS

**O Gláros €€** Mýrina, tel: 225 4 022. Straightforward fish *tavérna* overlooking Mýrina harbour and castle. Good wine, excellent service.

## LÉSVOS

**Averof €** Mytilíni town, where Ermoú Street meets the quay, tel: 225 102 2180. Founded by Greek refugees from Asia Minor and still run by the same family. These roots are evident in the good food.

# THE DODECANESE ISLANDS

## RHODES

**Alexis €€** 18 Sokrátes, Rhodes Town (old city), tel: 224 102 9347. Fine fresh fish served in the courtyard. Extensive wine list.
**Ta Kioúpia €€/€€€** 12 Argonáfton, Ixia, tel: 224 109 1824. Like Trýpas in Corfu, this beautiful restaurant charges a moderately high price for a seemingly endless supply of very good food.
**Mavríkos €€** Líndhos, tel: 224 403 1232. Excellent food, predominantly fish but also meat and vegetable dishes served politely in pleasant surroundings, on the square. A real treat.

## KÓS

**Hamam €€** 3 Nikíta Nissýrou Street, Diagóra Square, Kós Town. A beautifully restored building, once a *hammam*. This restaurant has some interesting Byzantine dishes. Good wines, polite service.

## PÁTMOS

**The Old Harbour €/€€** On harbour road in the centre of Skála, tel: 224 703 1170. Fresh fish, lobster, 'international' and Greek cooking on a verandah overlooking the seafront. Rightly popular.

# CRETE

**Ionía €** 3 Evans Street, Iráklio, behind the courthouse. Wide variety of oven- and casserole-cooked Greek and Cretan dishes.
**Avlí €€** Corner of Xánthoudidou and Radamánthios Streets, Réthymno (in the old town), tel: 283 102 6213. Wonderful selection of Cretan dishes served in a beautifully restored Venetian house.

# INDEX